MAKING *the* BEST CASE

Lessons in Writing from the World of Law

JEFF JUNG

Kendall Hunt
publishing company

Cover image © Shutterstock, Inc. Used under license.

Kendall Hunt
publishing company

www.kendallhunt.com
Send all inquiries to:
4050 Westmark Drive
Dubuque, IA 52004-1840

Copyright © 2011 by Jeff Jung

ISBN 978-0-7575-9090-0

Printed in the United States of America
10 9 8 7 6 5 4 3

To Mom & Dad, who made me who I am

To José & Logan, who lift me up

Contents

Preface

Why use examples from the world of law to learn how to write a college essay? There are many reasons. Law and language are intimately related. For at least 4,000 years, the law has depended on writing for its very existence, and in no other form of writing is every choice of words, syntax, and punctuation likely to be so ferociously and tirelessly debated. The attorney who cannot organize his argument and find the right evidence to support it will lose his case. The litigant who cannot tell his story clearly will win no supporters, and the law-maker who chooses his words poorly or writes without logic can unleash terrible injustice on the world for generations. By the power of language, rights are given or taken away, people are sent to jail, millions of dollars are awarded, families are altered, and the rules by which we live are determined.

By considering what goes on within the courtroom, we will observe principles that create effective writing and apply them to the task of writing the college essay. Doing so will allow us exciting opportunities to write about important matters, to see exactly how reasoning through writing affects ordinary lives, and to understand a bit about the law on the way. As you will see, the person who cannot read well is defenseless in any society governed by the rule of law.

That said, this book is not intended to teach you how to practice law. The examples and definitions given are not the actual laws of any government in particular; rather, they are based on the dominant trends found in the laws of the fifty states of the United States. This means that though you cannot quote this book in a courtroom or rely on it for legal advice, working through its activities will give you a good, general idea of how the law operates and how court decisions are made.

I wrote this book with a few goals in mind. I wanted to free students from the burden of writing about topics that they found difficult to engage with. For many years, the majority of composition textbooks have offered readings designed to enhance a student's sense of identity, encourage introspection, and help writers express their individuality. These are extremely noble goals, and some instructors have done wonderful things with these books. Those who require a more pragmatic context in which to refine their writing skills are likely to have a hard time finding a textbook with an alternative approach. Like it or not, there is no one that the law does not touch. I have found that my students' interest level and commitment to prove their point of view through writing increases enormously when invited to write on topics such as those found in this book. Secondly, I wanted to create a straightforward, common-sense approach to writing without the emphasis on theoretical explanations that weigh down many textbooks. Students need models to follow and impetus to write more than they need lists of the goals of composition or the types and subdivisions of rhetorical modes. Thirdly, I wanted a book that reflects the reality of the digital age by eliminating countless pages of drills and exercises and instead referring students to the Internet to obtain more practice on concepts that they find difficult. When cyberspace offers an infinite number of interactive exercises, why devote costly printed pages to the same?

Almost every book in this field that hits the shelves touts itself as a new approach. I hope you will find that this one merits the distinction.

Table of Cases

The Elements of an Essay
Law Enforcement

THE THESIS STATEMENT

What is a thesis?

Artistic writing requires creativity and originality of form, but a college essay has a more practical purpose. Its parts should work together like a well-coordinated machine, and ease-of-access and navigability for the reader are more important than surprises. Our first object, then, is to get acquainted with the basic anatomy of a college essay and see its various components at work.

A college essay, given its relatively small scale, is founded on a single, specific concept known as a ***thesis.*** The thesis reflects the purpose of the entire piece, the main idea that is to be conveyed, the central argument. While a book-length work might be so complex that its thesis can't be expressed without several sentences, a paper written in college should feature a thesis that can be voiced in a single sentence.

What makes a good thesis?

Beginning writers aren't always sure exactly what does or doesn't pass for a thesis statement, so that will be our first concern.

A Good Thesis ...

Makes a claim about a topic that requires proof or demonstration (which your essay provides)

Goes beyond merely stating a fact or observation

Is specific enough to give a clear idea of the paper's scope

The importance of having an identifiable, valid thesis can't be emphasized enough. If your paper lacks a good thesis, the reader . . .

- won't know what question your essay is trying to answer
- won't know what to think about the facts you present
- won't know whether to agree or disagree
- will have no idea how to find a way through the organization of your paper

We'll read the following excellent essay about criminal justice and use it as an example of our continuing discussion.

"How criminal justice is a lot like McDonald's"

McDonaldization is a term created by sociologist George Ritzer (2000:1) to describe the "the process by which the principles of the fast-food restaurant are coming to dominate more and more sectors of American society as well as the rest of the world." It is a process that represents the culmination of numerous practices of 20th century America, including bureaucratization, scientific management, and assembly line production.

According to Ritzer, McDonaldization is made up of four elements:

1. Efficiency is "the optimum method for getting from one point to another" or for achieving some goal (Ritzer, 2000: 12). In the fast food industry, efficiency is imperative, as the term "fast" implies;

2. Calculability is "an emphasis on the quantitative aspects of products sold . . . and services offered . . . In McDonaldized systems, quantity has become equivalent to quality; a lot of something, or the quick delivery of it, means it must be good" (Ritzer, 2000: 12). In the fast food industry, more for your money is better than less for your money;

3. Predictability refers to "the assurance that products and services will be the same over time and in all locales" (Ritzer, 2000: 13). In the fast food industry, the goal is to make one's entire dining experience completely consistent with all previous visits; no matter where you go, the product will be exactly the same; and

4. Control means that many aspects of production and consumption are governed by strict rules and an emphasis on one way of doing things. In the fast food industry, control is often achieved through the use of nonhuman technology (Ritzer, 2000: 236).

Any institution, system, or in this case, network of agencies, that stresses efficiency, calculability, predictability, and control, can be thought of as McDonaldized. According to my own research, America's agencies of criminal justice (police, courts, and corrections) have been McDonaldized, which means they tend to be aimed at efficiency, calculability, predictability, and control, perhaps even more than justice.

EFFICIENCY AND CRIMINAL JUSTICE

The importance of efficiency in American criminal justice has always been stressed, perhaps never in our nation's history as in the past three decades. When agencies of criminal justice are more focused on controlling crime than assuring fairness and impartiality, efficiency of criminal justice becomes the most important value; informal processes such as plea bargaining are used in place of trials to expedite criminal justice operations and hold a larger proportion of criminals accountable for their criminal acts.

To the degree that cases move through the criminal justice network like an "assembly line," criminal justice practice is much like a fast-food production line. Modern criminal justice practice aims to be efficient, even at the cost of due process rights of defendants. As you saw in Chapter 1, most criminal justice resources go to police and corrections, with courts receiving the fewest resources. The result is that almost all convictions by courts are achieved through the assembly line process of plea bargaining; less than 10% are convicted in criminal trials.

Allegiance to efficiency can also be seen within each of the agencies of criminal justice, including police, courts, and corrections. With regard to policing, the increased use of directed and aggressive patrol techniques (including foot and bike patrol), as part of a problem-oriented policing strategy, provides evidence that law enforcement values efficiency. The zero tolerance policing in our nation's largest cities, aimed at eliminating small problems of disorder before they grow into large crime problems, is further evidence of an allegiance to efficiency. The shift from two- to one-man police cars based on the realization that one-man cars are just as effective as those occupied by two officers provides further evidence for the importance of efficiency in policing. Finally, the growth of technology in policing, from crime analysis and crime mapping, to fingerprinting and computers in squad cars, suggests that policing is much more focused on proactive strategies than it has been historically.

With regard to courts, the popularity of plea bargaining provides tremendous evidence for the significance of efficiency in American courts. The ideal of American justice is an adversarial process, whereby prosecutors and defense attorneys fight for the truth and justice in a contest at trial. Yet, an administrative system is in effect, as evidenced by the large use of plea bargaining in courts; these cases are handled informally in hallways and offices rather than in courtrooms. Instead of criminal trials where prosecutors and defense attorneys clash in an effort to determine the truth and do justice for all concerned parties, prosecutors, defense attorneys, and sometimes judges "shop" for "supermarket" justice through plea bargaining. Criminal trials are now the exception to the rule of plea bargaining. Plea bargaining achieves only one thing—a more efficient court. Most criminologists and criminal justice scholars view plea bargaining as an unjust process driven by large numbers of caseloads, understaffed courts, and the renewed emphasis on using law enforcement to solve drug use and public order offenses (see Chapter 7).

With regard to corrections, a renewed emphasis on efficiency can be found in the increased use of incarceration to achieve incapacitation and deterrence of large numbers of inmates. Increased use of imprisonment is discussed below in the section on calculability. Here, it simply should be noted that a greater use of imprisonment implies to consumers that the criminal justice network will be more efficient in preventing crime because it will prevent criminality by those currently locked up and instill fear in those considering committing crimes.

Other evidence of increased efficiency in corrections includes legislative efforts to expedite executions by limiting appeals and the elimination of gain time and parole by states and the federal government. The elimination of gain time and parole is a major factor contributing to prison overcrowding.

Calculability and Criminal Justice

A greater emphasis has been placed on calculability in criminal justice over the past three decades—policy makers seem much more satisfied with more criminal justice (quantity) rather than better criminal justice (quality). Victimless crimes have at virtually all times in our nation's history been criminalized and we have fought numerous wars on drugs; yet, the most recent war on drugs under Presidents Reagan, Bush (the first), Clinton, and Bush (the second) has stressed much more criminal justice intervention than at any time in our nation's history. As a nation, we have spent more than $300 billion on the war on drugs since 1980; the cost of the drug war increased from just over $1 billion in federal dollars in the early 1980s to almost $20 billion in federal dollars in 2001. The largest portion of the 2001 figure (as in every previous year) was intended for domestic law enforcement while treatment and prevention received less than this and domestic social programs have been cut dramatically to pay for the war on drugs. The largest spending increases between the end of the Clinton presidency and the beginning of the Bush presidency (1996 and 2001) were for international spending and interdiction, while prevention and treatment increased less (see Chapter 11).

In policing, we see calculability in the promises by politicians to place more cops on the street and to build more prisons. We also see calculability in asset forfeitures in the nation's drug war. The reward for police is being allowed to confiscate and keep some drug-related assets, including cars, houses, cash, and other property. To some degree, law enforcement officials have come to rely on drug assets to purchase equipment and conduct training so that police can exterminate drug use. The majority of law enforcement agencies in the United States have asset forfeiture programs in place (see Chapter 6).

In courts, the value of calculability is seen in the passing of longer sentences for virtually all crimes. It is also evident in laws that require offenders to serve greater portions of their sentences—the so-called "truth in sentencing" laws (see Chapter 8).

In corrections, calculability means building more prisons, sending more people to prison, and a renewed use of capital punishment. The imprisonment rate in America has historically been relatively constant. It has fluctuated over the years, but never until the 1970s did it consistently and dramatically increase. Beginning in 1973, America began to engage in an imprisonment orgy (see Chapter 9). Since the early 1970s there has been approximately a 6.5% increase each year in imprisonment. Most of the increase has been due to drugs; from 1980 to 1993, the percentage of prisoners in state prisons serving sentences for drugs offenses more than tripled and in federal prisons more than doubled. America now has more than twice the rate of prisoners per 100,000 citizens as any other democracy, and more than 5 times the rate of democracies such as Canada, England, Germany, and France.

The ironic fact remains, however, that drug use trends have largely been unaffected since 1988 and drug abuse levels have always hovered at approximately the same level (see Chapter 11). An increased commitment to calculability—more criminal justice—has not resulted in substantial reductions in crime rates, nor drug use and abuse.

Predictability and Criminal Justice

If one were to fairly assess the performance of our nation's criminal justice network in terms of crime control over the past century, one could conclude that the likelihood of being subjected to it was always very unlikely; that is, the most predictable thing about it has been reactive criminal justice processes fail. Even today, the chance of being apprehended, convicted, and sentenced to imprisonment is highly unlikely for all crimes other than murder.

The most important factor in the effectiveness of deterrence is the certainty of punishment, that is, the likelihood of being punished. Research on deterrence has consistently found that the severity of a sentence has less of a deterrent effect than sentence certainty (see Chapter 8). American criminal justice performs poorly in providing certain, swift punishments that outweigh the potential benefits of committing crimes. Putting more cops on the street and increasing the use or prison sentences are efforts to make criminal justice outcomes more predictable.

In terms of policing, law enforcement officers now attempt to apprehend suspects by using offender profiling methods, which allows them to develop a picture of the offender based on elements of his or her crime. The scientific method has always been a part of policing, yet only in the past two decades, however, has offender profiling been used by police.

Police also try to accurately predict who is likely to get into trouble with the law before they commit criminal acts. They focus on particular types of people because of their own personal experience or that of their institution and profession, which suggests that certain people are more likely to violate the law. This practice, known as police profiling, results in startling disparities in police behavior based on class and race. Police use race, ethnicity, gender, and so forth, as a proxy for risk (see Chapter 6). Using race to establish probable cause is even supported by courts as legitimate when race is used in conjunction with other factors. Courts have stated that as long as the totality of the circumstances warrants the conclusion of the officer that the subject was acting suspiciously, race can be part of the circumstances considered by the officer. These elements of predictability in policing lead to difficulties in police-minority interactions, disproportionate use force against people of color, and disrespect for the law generally.

American courts are also highly predictable in all they do. The main actors in this process within the criminal courts—the prosecutor, the defense attorney, and the judge—enter the courtroom daily knowing essentially what will happen each day before it happens. Ideally, each member of the courtroom workgroup serves its own roles and has its own goals; in reality, each member's main job is not to rock the boat in the daily operations of America's courts.

Because of the strong working interpersonal relationships among courthouse workers, going rates are established in bail and sentencing. The process of plea bargaining, discussed earlier, serves as an excellent example. In studies of plea bargaining, cases are disposed of with great regularity and predictability meaning that the resulting sentence is reliably predicted based on the nature of the charges and the defendant's prior record. A going rate is established for particular types of crimes committed by particular types of people, one which becomes established over time and which is learned by each member of the courtroom workgroup. Plea bargains typically closely parallel this going rate, and defendants charged with particular crimes can easily learn what sentence they likely face if they plead guilty (see Chapter 7).

At the sentencing phase of courts, criminal penalties are highly predictable. Generally, the most important factors include the seriousness of the offense and the offender's prior record, so that the more serious the offense and the longer the prior record, the more severe the sentence will be. Mandatory sentences now establish a minimum sanction that must be served upon a conviction for a criminal offense. Thus, everyone who is convicted for a crime that calls for a mandatory sentence will serve that amount of time. Indeterminate sentences which allowed parole and determinate prison sentences which could be reduced by good-time or earned-time credits have been replaced by mandatory sentences across the country. Furthermore, sentencing guidelines have been established to make sentences more predictable and scientific based on a set of criteria including prior record, offense seriousness, and previous interactions with agencies of criminal justice. Sentencing grids reduce the discretion of judges and thus shift power to government prosecutors (see Chapter 8).

The best example of mandatory sentences are the "three strikes" laws in effect in more than half of our states. The logic of three strikes laws is to increase penalties of second offenses and require life imprisonment without possibility of parole for third offenses (see Chapter 8). These laws usually do not allow sentencing courts to consider particular circumstances of a crime, the duration of time that has elapsed between crimes, and mitigating factors in the background of offenders. The offender's potential for rehabilitation, ties to community, employment status, and obligations to children are also not taken into account.

Risk classification in corrections entails a great degree of prediction, as well. Individuals convicted of crimes can be put on probation, incarcerated in jail or prison, or subjected to some intermediate sanction; largely one's punishment is determined by offense seriousness, prior record, and behavior during previous criminal justice interventions. Yet, each form of punishment entails more or less supervision and fewer or greater rules to follow (e.g., probation versus intensive supervision probation), and/or greater restrictions on movement and activities (e.g., minimum versus maximum security) (see Chapter 9). The most violent and/or unmanageable inmates are now placed in isolation or incarcerated for 23 hours of the day in supermax prisons. These issues are discussed in the section on control that follows.

Control and Criminal Justice

As you saw in Chapter 1, in the past three decades, America has witnessed a rapid expansion of American criminal justice. This is evidence of increased control efforts by the criminal justice network and is criticized for being a disinvestment in the nation's future.

This expansion is literally unparalleled in history; yet corresponding decreases in crime have not been achieved. Indeed, street crime decreased throughout the 1990s but only about one-fourth of this decrease is attributable to imprisonment (see Chapter 4). The clearest control issue in criminal justice revolves around corrections. Correctional facilities are now state of art in terms of their use of technology to manage inmates. Increased use of other technologies include electronic monitoring of offenders under house arrest. Supermax prisons are the epitome of control. Offenders in super-maximum prisons have restricted contact with other inmates and with correctional personnel. Many inmates are locked in their cells for most of the day, in stark cells with white walls and bright lights on at all hours of day and night. Cells have completely closed front doors and no windows. In these prisons, prisoners are confined to their cells for 23 hours per day and can only take showers 2–3 times per week. When inmates are transferred, they are shackled in handcuffs and sometimes leg irons. Temperatures inside these facilities consistently register in the 80s and 90s.

The supermax facility gives us another interesting parallel between criminal justice and the fast food industry. Technically, nothing can be more maximum than "maximum" custody, yet now we have supermax custody. In fast food, french fries used to come in small, medium, and large. Now they come in medium, large, and extra large; the extra large sizes are "super sized," "biggie sized," and even "super super sized" and "great biggie sized." French fries provide the fast food industry their greatest profit margins for any of their products. The McDonaldized fast food industry tricks consumers to pay very high prices for a very small portion of one potato using deceptive terms such as "super super sized" and "great biggie sized" to convince consumers they are getting a good deal; the McDonaldized criminal justice network creates the illusion through the term supermax custody that these institutions keep Americans safe. In fact, most supermax inmates will one day be released back into society, having to readjust to even living with other people. And the costs to taxpayers just to build such facilities can be more than $130,000 per inmate.

From the analysis presented, it is clear that our criminal justice network has fallen victim to McDonaldization. Each aims to be as efficient and predictable as possible, each uses quantity as an evaluative criterion, and each is highly controlling. Given the frequency of exposure to the efficiency, calculability, predictability, and control of the fast food environment, people have probably come to expect these qualities from many institutions and services other than fast food restaurants.

This would make it easier for politicians to tout and sell fast and easy solutions to the nation's crime problem. Unfortunately, as American police, courts, and corrections have become McDonaldized, irrational policies have resulted. Although there is more criminal justice today than thirty years ago, although much of criminal justice practice is now highly predictable, and although Americans may now believe they are safer because of more control over criminals exerted by the government, the truth is that Americans are less sure of receiving justice from their agencies of criminal justice.

Identifying a thesis statement

Which sentence from the "McDonaldization" essay contains the thesis?

Thesis from "McDonaldization" Essay

According to my own research, America's agencies of criminal justice (police, courts, and corrections) have been McDonaldized, which means they tend to be aimed at efficiency, calculability, predictability, and control, perhaps even more than justice.

This thesis satisfies all three requirements we mentioned previously. It is a ***claim that requires proof,*** since readers will not automatically accept these charges against the justice system without hearing the details of the argument to follow. As such, it is ***not a mere statement of facts.*** Furthermore, it is ***highly specific,*** since the writer has identified precisely what sorts of accusations he wants to explore.

Here are some alternative thesis statements that would have been much weaker.

This Thesis Statement…	Is Weak Because…
Government systems have been McDonaldized, which means they tend to be aimed at efficiency, calculability, predictability, and control, perhaps even more than justice.	This is not specific enough. How can one paper cover all "government systems"? A country has not even been specified. The writer needs to narrow down to something more specific.
Government systems are full of problems.	This is nowhere near specific enough. Furthermore, we are crossing the line into "statement of fact." Everyone knows that government systems (like any systems) are full of problems.
The largest spending increases between the end of the Clinton presidency and the beginning of the Bush presidency (1996 and 2001) were for international spending and interdiction, while prevention and treatment increased less.	This is a statement of fact. To verify it, one would not read the following essay but would instead simply look it up. We want a thesis statement that invites the reader to read the essay.
McDonaldization is a term created by sociologist George Ritzer to describe "the process by which the principles of the fast-food restaurant are coming to dominate more and more sectors of American society as well as the rest of the world."	This is a statement of fact. It also could not serve as a thesis statement to this essay because the essay is not primarily about the term, "McDonaldization." It is primarily about the justice system, and "McDonaldization" is only a term (although an important one) used in the discussion. It is not the anchor of the essay as a whole.

ROADMAP

What is a roadmap?

In addition to delivering the thesis, the essay's first paragraph plays one other crucial role. It lets us know how the remainder of the essay will be organized, giving a **roadmap** that shows how each piece of the essay will play a part in proving the thesis.

Here, the roadmap indicates that we will look at how the negative effects of 1) efficiency, 2) calculabilty, 3) predictability, and 4) control all can be found in the American justice system. The reader now, instead of plunging into a mass of facts and details, knows where to find the logical divisions of the essay and understands how each part relates back to this central, guiding idea.

This writer was actually able to roll the roadmap right into the same sentence as the thesis itself. This is ideal, for it helps ensure that your thesis will be focused and specific. It may well lead to an extremely long sentence that, though something to be avoided as a general rule, is reasonable enough considering how important the thesis statement is. If, in fact, you can't make it all fit, it's not so bad to have the roadmap occupy the sentence or sentences right after the thesis.

Reviewing the thesis and the roadmap

Before moving on, let's do one more thing with this essay. Reread the section entitled "Calculability and Criminal Justice" and imagine that this were an essay all by itself. We'll call it a mini-essay. Which sentence contains the thesis of this mini-essay?

Write the thesis of the "Calculability" mini-essay in the space below.

_____

Now consider the following questions:

1. What does the roadmap in the first paragraph suggest will be the topics discussed in the rest of the mini-essay?

2. Where do you see those topics mentioned in the remainder of the mini-essay?

3. Once each topic is mentioned, what does the writer do in the rest of that paragraph before moving on to the next topic?

PARAGRAPH STRUCTURE AND TOPIC SENTENCES

What is a topic sentence?

Many students see paragraphs as arbitrary divisions they have to make so their essay will end up in five blocks. In fact, there is no specific number of paragraphs for an essay. A valid essay paragraph is a set of sentences devoted to a unified purpose—one step in the execution of the overall proof of the thesis. Once that purpose has been fulfilled, it's time to start a new paragraph.

Just as an essay is built upon a single thesis, each paragraph is built upon a ***topic sentence.*** This topic sentence is best placed at the front of the paragraph and should do two things:

Functions of the Topic Sentence

1. State the central idea that the remainder of the paragraph is going to support
2. Provide a direct connection back to the essay's thesis

Ideally, each topic sentence will relate to one element of the roadmap for the ultimate in user-friendliness. It is as if the roadmap were a series of hyperlinks with each element linking to a different topic sentence.

A paragraph should only attempt to perform one task in the grand scheme of the essay, and that task is the one named in the topic sentence. When reviewing your essay, you must interrogate each and every sentence. Is it really working to support the topic sentence? Is it providing new information as opposed to repeating old information? If either answer is no, that sentence does not deserve to be in the paragraph. Strike it.

Analyzing a topic sentence and its paragraph

We'll apply those criteria now to the fourth paragraph of the "Calculability and Criminal Justice" mini-essay. The topic sentence there is . . .

Topic Sentence of Paragraph 4 of "Calculability" Mini-Essay

"In corrections, calculability means building more prisons, sending more people to prison, and a renewed use of capital punishment."

Looking at the two functions of the topic sentence, we see that it does 1) state the central idea that the remainder of the paragraph supports. Everything else in the paragraph provides detailed evidence of the building of prisons, their increased use, and increased capital punishment. Does it also 2) provide a direct connection back to the essay's thesis? It does. The essay's thesis argues that an increase in quantity has been more important than quality in the criminal justice system. Clearly, the topic sentence bites off a piece of that argument by showing that it is true "in corrections." In the same way, the second and third paragraphs address other parts of the argument and reference them in their topic sentences: policing and courts.

How about the rest of the paragraph? Does every sentence relate to increased quantity of prisons, prisoners, and executions? Does every sentence add new detail without repetition? The answer is yes, making this a unified and supported paragraph.

1. Topic sentence establishes rising imprisonment as the central idea, and it relates to the "Corrections" part of the thesis.

2. Next two sentences note the original imprisonment rate.

3. Next sentence makes general claim that imprisonment rose.

4. Remaining sentences support the claim of rising imprisonment with various statistics.

Paragraph 4 of the "Calculability" Mini-Essay

In corrections, calculability means building more prisons, sending more people to prison, and a renewed use of capital punishment.[1] The imprisonment rate in America has historically been relatively constant. It has fluctuated over the years, but never until the 1970s did it consistently and dramatically increase.[2] Beginning in 1973, America began to engage in an imprisonment orgy (see Chapter 9).[3] Since the early 1970s there has been approximately a 6.5% increase each year in imprisonment. Most of the increase has been due to drugs; from 1980 to 1993, the percentage of prisoners in state prisons serving sentences for drugs offenses more than tripled and in federal prisons more than doubled. America now has more than twice the rate of prisoners per 100,000 citizens as any other democracy, and more than 5 times the rate of democracies such as Canada, England, Germany, and France.[4]

Thinking ahead: about support

Here's a thought for future consideration, however. Does it bother you that the writer hasn't told you where he got his information? In fact, this essay is just a preview of a larger work by the author, and he discusses the sources of his information later in the book. But if this excerpt had been a stand-alone essay you would be right to raise these objections. A college essay will always need to cite its sources to avoid giving the impression that the information is based on faulty authorities or even invented, as explained in Chapter 4.

Chapter

2

Thesis Statements
Wills · Evidence

RIGGS V. PALMER

Probate law: identifying the thesis of a case opinion

You've just seen the basic building blocks of an essay: thesis, road map, and topic sentences. We'll revisit these and see how and where they fit when we start to assemble our own essay in Chapter 4. For now, let's practice more with the concept of the thesis by looking at a legal decision considering a question of wills and murder.

Picking the thesis out of a piece of writing is usually rather easy when it is explicitly presented, as in the case of a college essay. But other forms of writing may be more subtle about their thesis, implying it rather than expressing it. Learning to recognize and express the thesis of someone else's writing is an important step in learning to formulate your own thesis statements and in analyzing complex documents. As you read the legal opinion that follows, ask yourself what seems to be the central argument that the judge is making.

Riggs v. Palmer

Court of Appeals of New York
115 N.Y. 506; 22 N.E. 188; (1889)

OPINION BY: EARL On the 13th day of August 1880, Francis B. Palmer made his last will and testament, in which he gave small legacies to his two daughters, Mrs. Riggs and Mrs. Preston, the plaintiffs in this action, and the remainder of his estate to his grandson, the defendant, Elmer E. Palmer * * * Elmer lived with him as a member of his family, and at his death was sixteen years old. He knew of the provisions made in his favor in the will, and, that he might prevent his grandfather from revoking such provisions, which he had manifested some intention to do, and to obtain the speedy enjoyment and

15

immediate possession of his property, he willfully murdered him by poisoning him. He now claims the property, and the sole question for our determination is, can he have it? The defendants say that the testator is dead; that his will was made in due form and has been admitted to probate, and that, therefore, it must have effect according to the letter of the law.

It is quite true that statutes regulating the making, proof and effect of wills, and the devolution of property, if literally construed, and if their force and effect can in no way and under no circumstances be controlled or modified, give this property to the murderer.

The purpose of those statutes was to enable testators to dispose of their estates to the objects of their bounty at death, and to carry into effect their final wishes legally expressed; and in considering and giving effect to them this purpose must be kept in view. It was the intention of the law-makers that the donees in a will should have the property given to them. But it never could have been their intention that a donee who murdered the testator to make the will operative should have any benefit under it. If such a case had been present to their minds, and it had been supposed necessary to make some provision of law to meet it, it cannot be doubted that they would have provided for it. * * * The writers of laws do not always express their intention perfectly, but either exceed it or fall short of it, so that judges are to collect it from probable or rational conjectures only, and this is called rational interpretation; and Rutherforth, in his Institutes (p. 407), says: "When we make use of rational interpretation, sometimes we restrain the meaning of the writer so as to take in less, and sometimes we extend or enlarge his meaning so as to take in more than his words express."

* * In 1 Blackstone's Commentaries (91) the learned author, speaking of the construction of statutes, says: "If there arise out of them any absurd consequences manifestly contradictory to common reason, they are, with regard to those collateral consequences, void. * * * When some collateral matter arises out of the general words, and happen to be unreasonable, then the judges are in decency to conclude that the consequence was not foreseen by the parliament, and, therefore, they are at liberty to . . . disregard it;"

There was a statute in Bologna that whoever drew blood in the streets should be severely punished, and yet it was held not to apply to the case of a barber who opened a vein in the street. It is commanded in the Decalogue [The Ten Commandments] that no work shall be done upon the Sabbath, and yet, giving the command a rational interpretation founded upon its design, the Infallible Judge [Jesus] held that it did not prohibit works of necessity, charity or benevolence on that day.

What could be more unreasonable than to suppose that it was the legislative intention in the general laws passed for the orderly, peaceable and just devolution of property, that they should have operation in favor of one who murdered his ancestor that he might speedily come into the possession of his estate? Such an intention is inconceivable. We need not, therefore, be much troubled by the general language contained in the laws.

Besides, all laws as well as all contracts may be controlled in their operation and effect by general, fundamental maxims of the common law. No one shall be permitted to profit by his own fraud, or to take advantage of his own wrong, or to found any claim upon his own iniquity, or to acquire property by his own crime. These maxims are dictated by public policy, have their foundation in universal law administered in all civilized countries, and have nowhere been superseded by statutes. . . .

* * If he had met the testator and taken his property by force, he would have had no title to it. Shall he acquire title by murdering him? If he had gone to the testator's house and by force compelled him, or by fraud or undue influence had induced him to will him his property, the law would not allow him to hold it. But can he give effect and operation to a will by murder, and yet take the property? To answer these questions in the affirmative, it seems to me, would be a reproach to the jurisprudence of our state, and an offense against public policy.

. . . . But, so far as I can find, in no country where the common law prevails has it been deemed important to enact a law to provide for such a case. Our revisers and lawmakers were familiar with the civil law, and they did not deem it important to incorporate into our statutes its provisions upon this subject. This is not a [case of omission]. It was evidently supposed that the maxims of the common law were sufficient to regulate such a case and that a specific enactment for that purpose was not needed.

For the same reasons the defendant Palmer cannot take any of this property as heir. Just before the murder he was not an heir, and it was not certain that he ever would be. He might have died before his grandfather, or might have been disinherited by him. He made himself an heir by the murder, and he seeks to take property as the fruit of his crime.

The judgment of the General Term and that entered upon the report of the referee should therefore be . . . that by reason of the crime of murder committed upon the grandfather [Elmer] is deprived of any interest in the estate left by him.

What would you say is the thesis of this writing? In other words, what argument did the writer want to prove? Write your response in the space that follows, and then compare it with the following variations and their evaluations.

Thesis for the Riggs v. Palmer case

Possible Thesis	Evaluation
Elmer's actions were immoral.	This does sound like a claim that requires proof and demonstration, but it is not the main argument that the writer wanted to prove. In fact, everyone probably already agrees that such a murder is immoral.
Murderers should not have rights.	This also sounds like a claim, but it is far too general. The writer wants to attack the rights of murderers to inherit, not strip all their rights.
No country has ever made a law specifying that murderers cannot profit from their crimes.	This is a statement of fact, not a claim requiring demonstration. Once the fact is verified, there is nothing left to prove or write about.
Some laws are difficult to interpret.	This is more like a claim but is extremely general. The writer is concerned with a very specific set of laws, not just "some laws." Also, he is more interested in arguing what the law should be rather than in proving that it's difficult to interpret.
Murderers should not be allowed to inherit property from their own victims.	This is the best variation here. It states a claim, not a fact, and is specific in identifying a certain class of criminals and exactly what it is that they should be prevented from doing.

THE PAVLINKO WILL

Probate law: identifying the thesis of a case opinion

Here's another case involving a will. What would you say is the thesis here?

In Re Pavlinko

The Supreme Court of Pennsylvania
394 Pa. 564; 148 A.2d 528 (1959)

OPINION: OPINION BY MR. JUSTICE BELL.

The facts are unusual and the result very unfortunate. Vasil Pavlinko and Hellen, his wife, retained a lawyer to draw their wills and wished to leave their property to each other. By mistake Hellen signed the will which was prepared for her husband, and Vasil signed the will which was prepared for his wife. . . . [After both Vasil and Hellen died, Hellen's brother, Elias Martin attempted to have the wills probated as he was listed in the wills as the sole beneficiary in the case of the death of both Vasil and Hellen. The probate court refused to recognize the validity of the wills due to the signature error, and Elias appealed.]

The Wills Act of 1947 provides in clear, plain and unmistakable language in § 2: "Every will shall be in writing and shall be signed *by the testator* at the end thereof" with certain exceptions not here relevant. The court below correctly held that the paper which *recited* that it was the will of Hellen Pavlinko and intended and purported to give Hellen's estate to her husband, could not be probated as the will of Vasil and was a nullity.

In order to decide in favor of the residuary legatee, almost the entire will would have to be rewritten. The court would have to substitute the words "Vasil Pavlinko" for "Hellen Pavlinko" and the words "my wife" wherever the words "my husband" appear in the will, and the relationship of the contingent residuary legatees would likewise have to be changed. To consider this paper—as written—as Vasil's will, it would give his entire residuary estate to "my husband, Vasil Pavlinko, absolutely" and "Third: If my husband, Vasil Pavlinko, should predecease me, then . . . I give and bequeath my residuary estate to my brother, Elias Martin." The language of this writing, which is signed at the end thereof by *Vasil* Pavlinko, is unambiguous, clear and unmistakable, and it is obvious that it is a meaningless nullity. . . .

Once a court starts to ignore or alter or rewrite or make exceptions to clear, plain and unmistakable provisions of the Wills Act in order to accomplish equity and justice in that particular case, the Wills Act will become a meaningless, although well intentioned, scrap of paper, and the door will be opened wide to countless fraudulent claims which the Act successfully bars.

***

Recalling our discussion of what makes a good thesis on page 1, we can form the following list of common problems with thesis statements.

Common Problems for Thesis Statements

1. States facts rather than makes a claim that requires proof/demonstration
2. Is not specific enough
3. Does not serve as the central focus for the essay

Compare the thesis that you identified for this case with the possibilities that follow. What problems do you see with them, if any? Which of the problems listed do you see in the possible thesis statements in the following table?

Possible Thesis	Evaluation
It is important to sign legal documents.	
Vasil and Hellen Pavlinko signed the wrong wills.	
The law must remain strict and not accept invalid wills just because it seems fair.	
It is highly unfortunate when a testator signs the wrong will.	
The Wills Act clearly requires that every will be signed by the testator.	

SOME DEFINITIONS: DIRECT AND CIRCUMSTANTIAL EVIDENCE

The following definitions will be useful in discussing the next two readings.

Direct Evidence: Evidence that is experienced firsthand, such as sights that a person saw himself or sounds that he heard himself. It is used directly, without the need of any other information, to help prove that something happened.

Circumstantial Evidence: Evidence that does not prove anything all by itself but that, when combined with common sense or other facts, can be used to prove something happened.

Examples
- If Mrs. Smith sees Bob shoot Tom, her testimony is direct evidence of Bob's murder of Tom.
- If she saw Bob enter Tom's room with a gun, heard a shot, and later entered to find Tom dead, this is only circumstantial evidence against Bob (i.e., common sense tells us he murdered Tom, but we have no direct proof).
- If Bob was heard yesterday stating that he wants Tom dead, this is direct evidence of his intentions.
- If Bob started finding a replacement for Tom yesterday, this is only circumstantial evidence suggesting that he might have had an intention to get rid of Tom—it's definitely not direct proof by itself.

LEO TOLSTOY'S "GOD SEES THE TRUTH BUT WAITS"

If you believe that authors of fiction have an idea they want to prove when they set out to write, then even stories can be seen as having a thesis. Read the following short story and see if you can infer a thesis. In other words, if the author were to substitute his story with a one-sentence argument, what would it be?

God Sees the Truth but Waits

by Leo Tolstoy

In the town of Vladimir lived a young merchant named Ivan Dmitrich Aksionov. He had two shops and a house of his own.

Aksionov was a handsome, fair-haired, curly-headed fellow, full of fun, and very fond of singing. When quite a young man he had been given to drink, and was riotous when he had had too much; but after he married he gave up drinking, except now and then.

One summer Aksionov was going to the Nizhny Fair, and as he bade good-bye to his family, his wife said to him, "Ivan Dmitrich, do not start to-day; I have had a bad dream about you."

Aksionov laughed, and said, "You are afraid that when I get to the fair I shall go on a spree."

His wife replied: "I do not know what I am afraid of; all I know is that I had a bad dream. I dreamt you returned from the town, and when you took off your cap I saw that your hair was quite grey."

Aksionov laughed. "That's a lucky sign," said he. "See if I don't sell out all my goods, and bring you some presents from the fair."

So he said good-bye to his family, and drove away.

When he had travelled half-way, he met a merchant whom he knew, and they put up at the same inn for the night. They had some tea together, and then went to bed in adjoining rooms.

It was not Aksionov's habit to sleep late, and, wishing to travel while it was still cool, he aroused his driver before dawn, and told him to put in the horses.

Then he made his way across to the landlord of the inn (who lived in a cottage at the back), paid his bill, and continued his journey.

When he had gone about twenty-five miles, he stopped for the horses to be fed. Aksionov rested awhile in the passage of the inn, then he stepped out into the porch, and, ordering a samovar to be heated, got out his guitar and began to play.

"God Sees the Truth But Waits" by Leo Tolstoy, 1872.

Suddenly a troika drove up with tinkling bells and an official alighted, followed by two soldiers. He came to Aksionov and began to question him, asking him who he was and whence he came. Aksionov answered him fully, and said, "Won't you have some tea with me?" But the official went on cross-questioning him and asking him. "Where did you spend last night? Were you alone, or with a fellow-merchant? Did you see the other merchant this morning? Why did you leave the inn before dawn?"

Aksionov wondered why he was asked all these questions, but he described all that had happened, and then added, "Why do you cross-question me as if I were a thief or a robber? I am travelling on business of my own, and there is no need to question me."

Then the official, calling the soldiers, said, "I am the police-officer of this district, and I question you because the merchant with whom you spent last night has been found with his throat cut. We must search your things."

They entered the house. The soldiers and the police-officer unstrapped Aksionov's luggage and searched it. Suddenly the officer drew a knife out of a bag, crying, "Whose knife is this?"

Aksionov looked, and seeing a blood-stained knife taken from his bag, he was frightened.

"How is it there is blood on this knife?"

Aksionov tried to answer, but could hardly utter a word, and only stammered: "I—don't know—not mine." Then the police-officer said: "This morning the merchant was found in bed with his throat cut. You are the only person who could have done it. The house was locked from inside, and no one else was there. Here is this blood-stained knife in your bag and your face and manner betray you! Tell me how you killed him, and how much money you stole?"

Aksionov swore he had not done it; that he had not seen the merchant after they had had tea together; that he had no money except eight thousand rubles of his own, and that the knife was not his. But his voice was broken, his face pale, and he trembled with fear as though he were guilty.

The police-officer ordered the soldiers to bind Aksionov and to put him in the cart. As they tied his feet together and flung him into the cart, Aksionov crossed himself and wept. His money and goods were taken from him, and he was sent to the nearest town and imprisoned there. Enquiries as to his character were made in Vladimir. The merchants and other inhabitants of that town said that in former days he used to drink and waste his time, but that he was a good man. Then the trial came on: he was charged with murdering a merchant from Ryazan, and robbing him of twenty thousand rubles.

His wife was in despair, and did not know what to believe. Her children were all quite small; one was a baby at her breast. Taking them all with her, she went to the town where her husband was in jail. At first she was not allowed to see him; but after much begging, she obtained permission from the officials, and was taken to him. When she saw her husband in prison-dress and in chains, shut up with thieves and criminals, she fell down, and did not come to her senses for a long time. Then she drew her children to her, and sat down near him. She told him of things at home, and asked about what had happened to him. He told her all, and she asked, "What can we do now?"

"We must petition the Czar not to let an innocent man perish."

His wife told him that she had sent a petition to the Czar, but it had not been accepted.

Aksionov did not reply, but only looked downcast.

Then his wife said, "It was not for nothing I dreamt your hair had turned grey. You remember? You should not have started that day." And passing her fingers through his hair, she said: "Vanya dearest, tell your wife the truth; was it not you who did it?"

"So you, too, suspect me!" said Aksionov, and, hiding his face in his hands, he began to weep. Then a soldier came to say that the wife and children must go away; and Aksionov said good-bye to his family for the last time.

When they were gone, Aksionov recalled what had been said, and when he remembered that his wife also had suspected him, he said to himself, "It seems that only God can know the truth; it is to Him alone we must appeal, and from Him alone expect mercy."

And Aksionov wrote no more petitions; gave up all hope, and only prayed to God.

Aksionov was condemned to be flogged and sent to the mines. So he was flogged with a knot, and when the wounds made by the knot were healed, he was driven to Siberia with other convicts.

For twenty-six years Aksionov lived as a convict in Siberia. His hair turned white as snow, and his beard grew long, thin, and grey. All his mirth went; he stooped; he walked slowly, spoke little, and never laughed, but he often prayed.

In prison Aksionov learnt to make boots, and earned a little money, with which he bought *The Lives of the Saints.* He read this book when there was light enough in the prison; and on Sundays in the prison-church he read the lessons and sang in the choir; for his voice was still good.

The prison authorities liked Aksionov for his meekness, and his fellow-prisoners respected him: they called him "Grandfather," and "The Saint." When they wanted to petition the prison authorities about anything, they always made Aksionov their spokesman, and when there were quarrels among the prisoners they came to him to put things right, and to judge the matter.

No news reached Aksionov from his home, and he did not even know if his wife and children were still alive.

One day a fresh gang of convicts came to the prison. In the evening the old prisoners collected round the new ones and asked them what towns or villages they came from, and what they were sentenced for. Among the rest Aksionov sat down near the newcomers, and listened with downcast air to what was said.

One of the new convicts, a tall, strong man of sixty, with a closely-cropped grey beard, was telling the others what he had been arrested for.

"Well, friends," he said, "I only took a horse that was tied to a sledge, and I was arrested and accused of stealing. I said I had only taken it to get home quicker, and had then let it go; besides, the driver was a personal friend of mine. So I said, 'It's all right.' 'No,' said they, 'you stole it.' But how or where I stole it they could not say. I once really did something wrong, and ought by rights to have come here long ago, but that time I was not found out. Now I have been sent here for nothing at all . . . Eh, but it's lies I'm telling you; I've been to Siberia before, but I did not stay long."

"Where are you from?" asked some one.

"From Vladimir. My family are of that town. My name is Makar, and they also call me Semyonich."

Aksionov raised his head and said: "Tell me, Semyonich, do you know anything of the merchants Aksionov of Vladimir? Are they still alive?"

"Know them? Of course I do. The Aksionovs are rich, though their father is in Siberia: a sinner like ourselves, it seems! As for you, Gran'dad, how did you come here?"

Aksionov did not like to speak of his misfortune. He only sighed, and said, "For my sins I have been in prison these twenty-six years."

"What sins?" asked Makar Semyonich.

But Aksionov only said, "Well, well—I must have deserved it!" He would have said no more, but his companions told the newcomers how Aksionov came to be in Siberia; how some one had killed a merchant, and had put the knife among Aksionov's things, and Aksionov had been unjustly condemned.

When Makar Semyonich heard this, he looked at Aksionov, slapped his *own* knee, and exclaimed, "Well, this is wonderful! Really wonderful! But how old you've grown, Gran'dad!"

The others asked him why he was so surprised, and where he had seen Aksionov before; but Makar Semyonich did not reply. He only said: "It's wonderful that we should meet here, lads!"

These words made Aksionov wonder whether this man knew who had killed the merchant; so he said, "Perhaps, Semyonich, you have heard of that affair, or maybe you've seen me before?"

"How could I help hearing? The world's full of rumours. But it's a long time ago, and I've forgotten what I heard."

"Perhaps you heard who killed the merchant?" asked Aksionov.

Makar Semyonich laughed, and replied: "It must have been him in whose bag the knife was found! If some one else hid the knife there, 'He's not a thief till he's caught,' as the saying is. How could any one put a knife into your bag while it was under your head? It would surely have woke you up."

When Aksionov heard these words, he felt sure this was the man who had killed the merchant. He rose and went away. All that night Aksionov lay awake. He felt terribly unhappy, and all sorts of images rose in his mind. There was the image of his wife as she was when he parted from her to go to the fair. He saw her as if she were present; her face and her eyes rose before him; he heard her speak and laugh. Then he saw his children, quite little, as they were at that time: one with a little cloak on, another at his mother's breast. And then he remembered himself as he used to be—young and merry. He remembered how he sat playing the guitar in the porch of the inn where he was arrested, and how free from care he had been. He saw, in his mind, the place where he was flogged, the executioner, and the people standing around; the chains, the convicts, all the twenty-six years of his prison life, and his premature old age. The thought of it all made him so wretched that he was ready to kill himself.

"And it's all that villain's doing!" thought Aksionov. And his anger was so great against Makar Semyonich that he longed for vengeance, even if he himself should perish for it. He kept repeating prayers all night, but could get no peace. During the day he did not go near Makar Semyonich, nor even look at him.

A fortnight passed in this way. Aksionov could not sleep at night, and was so miserable that he did not know what to do.

One night as he was walking about the prison he noticed some earth that came rolling out from under one of the shelves on which the prisoners slept. He stopped to see what it was. Suddenly Makar Semyonich crept out from under the shelf, and looked up at Aksionov with frightened face. Aksionov tried to pass without looking at him, but Makar seized his hand and told him that he had dug a hole under the wall, getting rid of the earth by putting it into his high-boots, and emptying it out every day on the road when the prisoners were driven to their work.

"Just you keep quiet, old man, and you shall get out too. If you blab, they'll flog the life out of me, but I will kill you first."

Aksionov trembled with anger as he looked at his enemy. He drew his hand away, saying, "I have no wish to escape, and you have no need to kill me; you killed me long ago! As to telling of you—I may do so or not, as God shall direct."

Next day, when the convicts were led out to work, the convoy soldiers noticed that one or other of the prisoners emptied some earth out of his boots. The prison was searched and the tunnel found. The Governor came and questioned all the prisoners to find out who had dug the hole. They all denied any knowledge of it. Those who knew would not betray Makar Semyonich, knowing he would be flogged almost to death. At last the Governor turned to Aksionov whom he knew to be a just man, and said:

"You are a truthful old man; tell me, before God, who dug the hole?"

Makar Semyonich stood as if he were quite unconcerned, looking at the Governor and not so much as glancing at Aksionov. Aksionov's lips and hands trembled, and for a long time he could not utter a word. He thought, "Why should I screen him who ruined my life? Let him pay for what I have suffered. But if I tell, they will probably flog the life out of him, and maybe I suspect him wrongly. And, after all, what good would it be to me?"

"Well, old man," repeated the Governor, "tell me the truth: who has been digging under the wall?"

Aksionov glanced at Makar Semyonich, and said, "I cannot say, your honour. It is not God's will that I should tell! Do what you like with me; I am in your hands."

However much the Governor tried, Aksionov would say no more, and so the matter had to be left.

That night, when Aksionov was lying on his bed and just beginning to doze, some one came quietly and sat down on his bed. He peered through the darkness and recognised Makar.

"What more do you want of me?" asked Aksionov. "Why have you come here?"

Makar Semyonich was silent. So Aksionov sat up and said, "What do you want? Go away, or I will call the guard!"

Makar Semyonich bent close over Aksionov, and whispered, "Ivan Dmitrich, forgive me!"

"What for?" asked Aksionov.

"It was I who killed the merchant and hid the knife among your things. I meant to kill you too, but I heard a noise outside, so I hid the knife in your bag and escaped out of the window."

Aksionov was silent, and did not know what to say. Makar Semyonich slid off the bed-shelf and knelt upon the ground. "Ivan Dmitrich," said he, "forgive me! For the love of God, forgive me! I will confess that it was I who killed the merchant, and you will be released and can go to your home."

"It is easy for you to talk," said Aksionov, "but I have suffered for you these twenty-six years. Where could I go to now? . . . My wife is dead, and my children have forgotten me. I have nowhere to go . . ."

Makar Semyonich did not rise, but beat his head on the floor. "Ivan Dmitrich, forgive me!" he cried. "When they flogged me with the knot it was not so hard to bear as it is to see you now . . . yet you had pity on me, and did not tell. For Christ's sake forgive me, wretch that I am!" And he began to sob.

When Aksionov heard him sobbing he, too, began to weep. "God will forgive you!" said he. "Maybe I am a hundred times worse than you." And at these words his heart grew light, and the longing for home left him. He no longer had any desire to leave the prison, but only hoped for his last hour to come.

In spite of what Aksionov had said, Makar Semyonich confessed his guilt. But when the order for his release came, Aksionov was already dead.

Identifying the thesis of a short story

Here, several possible thesis statements could be inferred. Write your evaluations of each thesis statement in the space provided. Remember the criteria: Is the statement a claim that requires proof and demonstration? Does it go beyond merely stating a fact? Is it specific? Is it really the foundation of the entire writing?

Possible Thesis Statement	Evaluation
Injustice results when a man can be convicted by circumstantial evidence (defined on page 20) instead of conclusive proof.	
Many convicted criminals turn out to be innocent.	
Aksionov suffered for many years in prison but was eventually able to find inner peace.	
Women should support their husbands no matter what their situation.	
The death penalty should be abolished since a murder conviction may turn out to be erroneous.	
Russia suffers from problems involving criminals.	
Guilt can be an even more powerful punishment than anything the government can inflict.	

EXCERPT FROM MELVILLE DAVISSON POST'S "THE CORPUS DELICTI"

In the short story, "The Corpus Delicti," Samuel Walcott (whose real name is Richard Warren) is being blackmailed by Nina San Croix because she is jealous of his upcoming marriage. She threatens to expose a murder that he committed many years ago, and so he decides to eliminate her by disguising himself as a Mexican sailor named Victor Ancona. As you read the story, determine what possible thesis could be inferred from it.

The Corpus Delicti

by Melville Davisson Post

The place which Samuel Walcott had selected for the residence of Nina San Croix was far up in the northern suburb of New York. The place was very old. The lawn was large and ill kept; the house, a square old-fashioned brick, was set far back from the street, and partly hidden by trees. Around it all was a rusty iron fence. The place had the air of genteel ruin, such as one finds in the Virginias.

On a Thursday of November, about three o'clock in the afternoon, a little man, driving a dray, stopped in the alley at the rear of the house. As he opened the back gate an old negro woman came down the steps from the kitchen and demanded to know what he wanted. The drayman asked if the lady of the house was in. The old negro answered that she was asleep at this hour and could not be seen.

"That is good," said the little man, "now there won't be any row. I brought up some cases of wine which she ordered from our house last week and which the Boss told me to deliver at once, but I forgot it until to-day. Just let me put it in the cellar now, Auntie, and don't say a word to the lady about it and she won't ever know that it was not brought up on time."

The drayman stopped, fished a silver dollar out of his pocket, and gave it to the old negro. "There now, Auntie," he said, "my job depends upon the lady not knowing about this wine; keep it mum."

"Dat's all right, honey," said the old servant, beaming like a May morning. "De cellar door is open, carry it all in and put it in de back part and nobody ain't never going to know how long it has been in dar."

The old negro went back into the kitchen and the little man began to unload the dray. He carried in five wine cases and stowed them away in the back part of the cellar

Excerpted from *The Corpus Delicti* by Melville Davisson Post, 1896.

as the old woman had directed. Then, after having satisfied himself that no one was watching, he took from the dray two heavy paper sacks, presumably filled with flour, and a little bundle wrapped in an old newspaper; these he carefully hid behind the wine cases in the cellar. After awhile he closed the door, climbed on his dray, and drove off down the alley.

About eight o'clock in the evening of the same day, a Mexican sailor dodged in the front gate and slipped down to the side of the house. He stopped by the window and tapped on it with his finger. In a moment a woman opened the door. She was tall, lithe, and splendidly proportioned, with a dark Spanish face and straight hair. The man stepped inside. The woman bolted the door and turned round.

"Ah," she said, smiling, "it is you, Señor? How good of you!"

The man started. "Whom else did you expect?" he said quickly.

"Oh!" laughed the woman, "perhaps the Archbishop."

"Nina!" said the man, in a broken voice that expressed love, humility, and reproach. His face was white under the black sunburn.

For a moment the woman wavered. A shadow flitted over her eyes, then she stepped back. "No," she said, "not yet."

The man walked across to the fire, sank down in a chair, and covered his face with his hands. The woman stepped up noiselessly behind him and leaned over the chair. The man was either in great agony or else he was a superb actor, for the muscles of his neck twitched violently and his shoulders trembled.

"Oh," he muttered, as though echoing his thoughts, "I can't do it, I can't!"

The woman caught the words and leaped up as though some one had struck her in the face. She threw back her head. Her nostrils dilated and her eyes flashed.

"You can't do it!" she cried. "Then you do love her! You shall do it! Do you hear me? You shall do it! You killed him! You got rid of him! but you shall not get rid of me. I have the evidence, all of it. The Archbishop will have it to-morrow. They shall hang you! Do you hear me? They shall hang you!"

The woman's voice rose, it was loud and shrill. The man turned slowly round without looking up, and stretched out his arms toward the woman. She stopped and looked down at him. The fire glittered for a moment and then died out of her eyes, her bosom heaved and her lips began to tremble. With a cry she flung herself into his arms, caught him around the neck, and pressed his face up close against her cheek.

"Oh! Dick, Dick," she sobbed, "I do love you so! I can't live without you! Not another hour, Dick! I do want you so much, so much, Dick!"

The man shifted his right arm quickly, slipped a great Mexican knife out of his sleeve, and passed his fingers slowly up the woman's side until he felt the heart beat under his hand, then he raised the knife, gripped the handle tight, and drove the keen blade into the woman's bosom. The hot blood gushed out over his arm, and down on his leg. The body, warm and limp, slipped down in his arms. The man got up, pulled out the knife, and thrust it into a sheath at his belt, unbuttoned the dress, and slipped it off of the body.

As he did this a bundle of papers dropped upon the floor; these he glanced at hastily and put into his pocket. Then he took the dead woman up in his arms, went out into the hall, and started to go up the stairway. The body was relaxed and heavy, and for that reason difficult to carry. He doubled it up into an awful heap, with the knees against the chin, and walked slowly and heavily up the stairs and out into the bathroom. There he laid the corpse down on the tiled floor. Then he opened the window, closed the shutters, and lighted the gas. The bathroom was small and contained an ordinary steel tub, porcelain lined, standing near the window and raised about six inches above the floor. The sailor went over to the tub, pried up the metal rim of the outlet with his knife, removed it, and fitted into its place a porcelain disk which he took from his pocket; to this disk was attached a long platinum wire, the end of which he fastened on the outside of the tub. After he had done this he went back to the body, stripped off its clothing, put it down in the tub and began to dismember it with the great Mexican knife. The blade was strong and sharp as a razor. The man worked rapidly and with the greatest care.

When he had finally cut the body into as small pieces as possible, he replaced the knife in its sheath, washed his hands, and went out of the bathroom and downstairs to the lower hall. The sailor seemed perfectly familiar with the house. By a side door he passed into the cellar. There he lighted the gas, opened one of the wine cases, and, taking up all the bottles that he could conveniently carry, returned to the bathroom. There he poured the contents into the tub on the dismembered body, and then returned to the cellar with the empty bottles, which he replaced in the wine cases. This he continued to do until all the cases but one were emptied and the bath tub was more than half full of liquid. This liquid was sulphuric acid.

When the sailor returned to the cellar with the last empty wine bottles, he opened the fifth case, which really contained wine, took some of it out, and poured a little into each of the empty bottles in order to remove any possible odor of the sulphuric acid. Then he turned out the gas and brought up to the bathroom with him the two paper flour sacks and the little heavy bundle. These sacks were filled with nitrate of soda. He set them down by the door, opened the little bundle, and took out two long rubber tubes, each attached to a heavy gas burner, not unlike the ordinary burners of a small gas stove. He fastened the tubes to two of the gas jets, put the burners under the tub, turned the gas on full, and lighted it. Then he threw into the tub the woman's clothing and the papers which he had found on her body, after which he took up the two heavy sacks of nitrate of soda and dropped them carefully into the sulphuric acid. When he had done this he went quickly out of the bathroom and closed the door.

The deadly acids at once attacked the body and began to destroy it; as the heat increased, the acids boiled and the destructive process was rapid and awful. From time to time the sailor opened the door of the bathroom cautiously, and, holding a wet towel over his mouth and nose, looked in at his horrible work. At the end of a few hours there was only a swimming mass in the tub. When the man looked at four o'clock, it was all a thick murky liquid. He turned off the gas quickly and stepped back out of the room. For perhaps half an hour he waited in the hall; finally, when the acids had cooled so that they no longer gave off fumes, he opened the door and went in, took hold of the platinum wire and, pulling the porcelain disk from the stopcock, allowed the awful contents of the tub to run out. Then he turned on the hot water, rinsed the tub clean, and replaced the metal outlet. Removing the rubber tubes, he cut them into pieces, broke the porcelain disk, and, rolling up the platinum wire, washed it all down the sewer pipe.

The fumes had escaped through the open window; this he now closed and set himself to putting the bathroom in order, and effectually removing every trace of his night's work. The sailor moved around with the very greatest degree of care. Finally, when he had arranged everything to his complete satisfaction, he picked up the two burners, turned out the gas, and left the bathroom, closing the door after him. From the bathroom he went directly to the attic, concealed the two rusty burners under a heap of rubbish, and then walked carefully and noiselessly down the stairs and through the lower hall. As he opened the door and stepped into the room where he had killed the woman, two police officers sprang out and seized him. The man screamed like a wild beast taken in a trap and sank down.

"Oh! oh!" he cried, "it was no use! it was no use to do it!" Then he recovered himself in a manner and was silent. The officers handcuffed him, summoned the patrol, and took him at once to the station house. There he said he was a Mexican sailor and that his name was Victor Ancona; but he would say nothing further. The following morning he sent for Randolph Mason and the two were long together.

IV

The obscure defendant charged with murder has little reason to complain of the law's delays. The morning following the arrest of Victor Ancona, the newspapers published long sensational articles, denounced him as a fiend, and convicted him. The grand jury, as it happened, was in session. The preliminaries were soon arranged and the case was railroaded into trial. The indictment contained a great many counts, and charged the prisoner with the murder of Nina San Croix by striking, stabbing, choking, poisoning, and so forth.

The trial had continued for three days and had appeared so overwhelmingly one-sided that the spectators who were crowded in the court room had grown to be violent and bitter partisans, to such an extent that the police watched them closely. The attorneys for the People were dramatic and denunciatory, and forced their case with arrogant confidence. Mason, as counsel for the prisoner, was indifferent and listless. Throughout the entire trial he had sat almost motionless at the table, his gaunt form bent over, his long legs drawn up under his chair, and his weary, heavy-muscled face, with its restless eyes, fixed and staring out over the heads of the jury, was like a tragic mask. The bar, and even the judge, believed that the prisoner's counsel had abandoned his case.

The evidence was all in and the People rested. It had been shown that Nina San Croix had resided for many years in the house in which the prisoner was arrested; that she had lived by herself, with no other companion than an old negro servant; that her past was unknown, and that she received no visitors, save the Mexican sailor, who came to her house at long intervals. Nothing whatever was shown tending to explain who the prisoner was or whence he had come. It was shown that on Tuesday preceding the killing the Archbishop had received a communication from Nina San Croix, in which she said she desired to make a statement of the greatest import, and asking for an audience. To this the Archbishop replied that he would willingly grant her a hearing if she would come to him at eleven o'clock on Friday morning. Two policemen testified that about eight o'clock on the night of Thursday they had noticed the prisoner slip into the gate of Nina San Croix's residence and go down to the side of the house, where he was admitted; that his appearance and seeming haste had attracted their attention; that they had concluded that it was some clandestine amour, and out of curiosity had both slipped down to the house and endeavored to find a position from which they could see into the room, but were unable to do so, and were about to go back to the street when they heard a woman's voice cry out in, great anger: "I know that you love her and that you want to get rid of me, but you shall not do it! You murdered him, but you shall not murder me! I have all the evidence to convict you of murdering him! The Archbishop will have it tomorrow! They shall hang you! Do you hear me? They shall hang you for this murder!" that thereupon one of the policemen proposed that they should break into the house and see what was wrong, but the other had urged that it was only the usual lovers' quarrel and if they should interfere they would find nothing upon which a charge could be based and would only be laughed at by the chief; that they had waited and listened for a time, but hearing nothing further had gone back to the street and contented themselves with keeping a strict watch on the house.

The People proved further, that on Thursday evening Nina San Croix had given the old negro domestic a sum of money and dismissed her, with the instruction that she was not to return until sent for. The old woman testified that she had gone directly to the house of her son, and later had discovered that she had forgotten some articles of clothing which she needed; that thereupon she had returned to the house and had gone up the back way to her room,—this was about eight o'clock; that while there she had heard Nina San Croix's voice in great passion and remembered that she had used the words stated by the policemen; that these sudden, violent cries had frightened her greatly and she had bolted the door and been afraid to leave the room; shortly thereafter, she had heard heavy footsteps ascending the stairs, slowly and with great difficulty, as though some one were carrying a heavy burden; that therefore her fear had increased and that she had put out the light and hidden under the bed. She remembered hearing the footsteps moving about upstairs for many hours, how long she could not tell. Finally, about half-past four in the morning, she crept out, opened the door, slipped downstairs, and ran out into the street. There she had found the policemen and requested them to search the house.

The two officers had gone to the house with the woman. She had opened the door and they had had just time to step back into the shadow when the prisoner entered. When arrested, Victor Ancona had screamed with terror, and cried out, "It was no use! it was no use to do it!"

The Chief of Police had come to the house and instituted a careful search. In the room below, from which the cries had come, he found a dress which was identified as belonging to Nina San Croix and which she was wearing when last seen by the domestic, about six o'clock that evening. This dress was covered with blood, and had a slit about two inches long in the left side of the bosom, into which the Mexican knife, found on the prisoner, fitted perfectly. These articles were introduced in evidence, and it was shown that the slit would be exactly over the heart of the wearer, and that such a wound would certainly result in death. There was much blood on one of the chairs and on the floor. There was also blood on the prisoner's coat and the leg of his trousers, and the heavy Mexican knife was also bloody. The blood was shown by the experts to be human blood.

The body of the woman was not found, and the most rigid and tireless search failed to develop the slightest trace of the corpse, or the manner of its disposal. The body of the woman had disappeared as completely as though it had vanished into the air.

When counsel announced that he had closed for the People, the judge turned and looked gravely down at Mason. "Sir," he said, "the evidence for the defense may now be introduced."

Randolph Mason arose slowly and faced the judge.

"If your Honor please," he said, speaking slowly and distinctly, "the defendant has no evidence to offer." He paused while a murmur of astonishment ran over the court room. "But, if your Honor please," he continued, "I move that the jury be directed to find the prisoner not guilty."

The crowd stirred. The counsel for the People smiled. The judge looked sharply at the speaker over his glasses. "On what ground?" he said curtly.

"On the ground," replied Mason, "that the corpus delicti has not been proven."

"Ah!" said the judge, for once losing his judicial gravity. Mason sat down abruptly. The senior counsel for the prosecution was on his feet in a moment.

"What!" he said, "the gentleman bases his motion on a failure to establish the corpus delicti? Does he jest, or has he forgotten the evidence? The term 'corpus delicti' is technical, and means the body of the crime, or the substantial fact that a crime has been committed. Does anyone doubt it in this case? It is true that no one actually saw the prisoner kill the decedent, and that he has so successfully hidden the body that it has not been found, but the powerful chain of circumstances, clear and close-linked, proving motive, the criminal agency, and the criminal act, is overwhelming.

"The victim in this case is on the eve of making a statement that would prove fatal to the prisoner. The night before the statement is to be made he goes to her residence. They quarrel. Her voice is heard, raised high in the greatest passion, denouncing him, and charging that he is a murderer, that she has the evidence and will reveal it, that he shall be hanged, and that he shall not be rid of her. Here is the motive for the crime, clear as light. Are not the bloody knife, the bloody dress, the bloody clothes of the prisoner, unimpeachable witnesses to the criminal act? The criminal agency of the prisoner has not the shadow of a possibility to obscure it. His motive is gigantic. The blood on him, and his despair when arrested, cry 'Murder! murder!' with a thousand tongues.

"Men may lie, but circumstances cannot. The thousand hopes and fears and passions of men may delude, or bias the witness. Yet it is beyond the human mind to conceive that a clear, complete chain of concatenated circumstances can be in error. Hence it is that the greatest jurists have declared that such evidence, being rarely liable to delusion or fraud, is safest and most powerful. The machinery of human justice cannot guard against the remote and improbable doubt. The inference is persistent in the affairs of men. It is the only means by which the human mind reaches the truth. If you forbid the jury to exercise it, you bid them work after first striking off their hands. Rule out the irresistible inference, and the end of justice is come in this land; and you may as well leave the spider to weave his web through the abandoned court room."

The attorney stopped, looked down at Mason with a pompous sneer, and retired to his place at the table. The judge sat thoughtful and motionless. The jurymen leaned forward in their seats.

"If your Honor please," said Mason, rising, "this is a matter of law, plain, clear, and so well settled in the State of New York that even counsel for the People should know it. The question before your Honor is simple. If the corpus delicti, the body of the crime, has been proven, as required by the laws of the commonwealth, then this case should go to the jury. If not, then it is the duty of this Court to direct the jury to find the prisoner not guilty. There is here no room for judicial discretion. Your Honor has but to recall and apply the rigid rule announced by our courts prescribing distinctly how the corpus delicti in murder must be proven.

"The prisoner here stands charged with the highest crime. The law demands, first, that the crime, as a fact, be established. The fact that the victim is indeed dead must first be made certain before anyone can be convicted for her killing, because, so long as there remains the remotest doubt as to the death, there can be no certainty as to the criminal agent, although the circumstantial evidence indicating the guilt of the accused may be positive, complete, and utterly irresistible. In murder, the corpus delicti, or body of the crime, is composed of two elements:

"Death, as a result.

"The criminal agency of another as the means.

It is the fixed and immutable law of this State, laid down in the leading case of Ruloff v. The People, and binding upon this Court, that both components of the corpus delicti shall not be established by circumstantial evidence. There must be direct proof of one or the other of these two component elements of the corpus delicti. If one is proven by direct evidence, the other may be presumed; but both shall not be presumed from circumstances, no matter how powerful, how cogent, or how completely overwhelming the circumstances may be. In other words, no man can be convicted of murder in the State of New York, unless the body of the victim be found and identified, or there be direct proof that the prisoner did some act adequate to produce death, and did it in such a manner as to account for the disappearance of the body."

The face of the judge cleared and grew hard. The members of the bar were attentive and alert; they were beginning to see the legal escape open up. The audience were puzzled; they did not yet understand. Mason turned to the counsel for the People. His ugly face was bitter with contempt.

"For three days," he said, "I have been tortured by this useless and expensive farce. If counsel for the People had been other than play-actors, they would have known in the beginning that Victor Ancona could not be convicted for murder, unless he were confronted in this court room with a living witness, who had looked into the dead face of Nina San Croix; or, if not that, a living witness who had seen him drive the dagger into her bosom.

"I care not if the circumstantial evidence in this case were so strong and irresistible as to be overpowering; if the judge on the bench, if the jury, if every man within sound of my voice, were convinced of the guilt of the prisoner to the degree of certainty that is absolute; if the circumstantial evidence left in the mind no shadow of the remotest improbable doubt; yet, in the absence of the eyewitness, this prisoner cannot be punished, and this Court must compel the jury to acquit him."

The audience now understood, and they were dumfounded. Surely this was not the law. They had been taught that the law was common sense, and this,—this was anything else.

Mason saw it all, and grinned. "In its tenderness," he sneered, "the law shields the innocent. The good law of New York reaches out its hand and lifts the prisoner out of the clutches of the fierce jury that would hang him."

Mason sat down. The room was silent. The jurymen looked at each other in amazement. The counsel for the People arose. His face was white with anger, and incredulous.

"Your Honor," he said, "this doctrine is monstrous. Can it be said that, in order to evade punishment, the murderer has only to hide or destroy the body of the victim, or sink it into the sea? Then, if he is not seen to kill, the law is powerless and the murderer can snap his finger in the face of retributive justice. If this is the law, then the law for the highest crime is a dead letter. The great commonwealth winks at murder and invites every man to kill his enemy, provided he kill him in secret and hide him. I repeat, your Honor,"—the man's voice was now loud and angry and rang through the court room— "that this doctrine is monstrous!"

"So said Best, and Story, and many another," muttered Mason, "and the law remained."

"The Court," said the judge, abruptly, "desires no further argument."

The counsel for the People resumed his seat. His face lighted up with triumph. The Court was going to sustain him.

The judge turned and looked down at the jury. He was grave, and spoke with deliberate emphasis.

"Gentlemen of the jury," he said, "the rule of Lord Hale obtains in this State and is binding upon me. It is the law as stated by counsel for the prisoner: that to warrant conviction of murder there must be direct proof either of the death, as of the finding and identification of the corpse, or of criminal violence adequate to produce death, and exerted in such a manner as to account for the disappearance of the body; and it is only when there is direct proof of the one that the other can be established by circumstantial evidence. This is the law, and cannot now be departed from. I do not presume to explain its wisdom. Chief Justice Johnson has observed, in the leading case, that it may have its probable foundation in the idea that where direct proof is absent as to both the fact of the death and of criminal violence capable of producing death, no evidence can rise to the degree of moral certainty that the individual is dead by criminal intervention, or even lead by direct inference to this result; and that, where the fact of death is not certainly ascertained, all inculpatory circumstantial evidence wants the key necessary for its satisfactory interpretation, and cannot be depended on to furnish more than probable results. It may be, also, that such a rule has some reference to the dangerous possibility that a general preconception of guilt, or a general excitement of popular feeling, may creep in to supply the place of evidence, if, upon other than direct proof of death or a cause of death, a jury are permitted to pronounce a prisoner guilty.

"In this case the body has not been found and there is no direct proof of criminal agency on the part of the prisoner, although the chain of circumstantial evidence is complete and irresistible in the highest degree. Nevertheless, it is all circumstantial evidence, and under the laws of New York the prisoner cannot be punished. I have no right of discretion. The law does not permit a conviction in this case, although every one of us may be morally certain of the prisoner's guilt. I am, therefore, gentlemen of the jury, compelled to direct you to find the prisoner not guilty."

"Judge," interrupted the foreman, jumping up in the box, "we cannot find that verdict under our oath; we know that this man is guilty."

"Sir," said the judge, "this is a matter of law in which the wishes of the jury cannot be considered. The clerk will write a verdict of not guilty, which you, as foreman, will sign."

The spectators broke out into a threatening murmur that began to grow and gather volume. The judge rapped on his desk and ordered the bailiffs promptly to suppress any demonstration on the part of the audience. Then he directed the foreman to sign the verdict prepared by the clerk. When this was done he turned to Victor Ancona; his face was hard and there was a cold glitter in his eyes.

"Prisoner at the bar," he said, "you have been put to trial before this tribunal on a charge of cold-blooded and atrocious murder. The evidence produced against you was of such powerful and overwhelming character that it seems to have left no doubt in the minds of the jury, nor indeed in the mind of any person present in this court room.

"Had the question of your guilt been submitted to these twelve arbiters, a conviction would certainly have resulted and the death penalty would have been imposed. But the law, rigid, passionless, even-eyed, has thrust in between you and the wrath of your fellows and saved you from it. I do not cry out against the impotency of the law; it is perhaps as wise as imperfect humanity could make it. I deplore, rather, the genius of evil men who, by cunning design, are enabled to slip through the fingers of this law. I have no word of censure or admonition for you, Victor Ancona. The law of New York compels me to acquit you. I am only its mouthpiece, with my individual wishes throttled. I speak only those things which the law directs I shall speak.

"You are now at liberty to leave this court room, not guiltless of the crime of murder, perhaps, but at least rid of its punishment. The eyes of men may see Cain's mark on your brow, but the eyes of the Law are blind to it."

When the audience fully realized what the judge had said they were amazed and silent. They knew as well as men could know, that Victor Ancona was guilty of murder, and yet he was now going out of the court room free. Could it happen that the law protected only against the blundering rogue? They had heard always of the boasted completeness of the law which magistrates from time immemorial had labored to perfect, and now when the skillful villain sought to evade it, they saw how weak a thing it was.

Possible Thesis	Evaluation
Courts should consider indirect evidence as well as direct evidence, or else an obviously guilty person could go free.	
Samuel Walcott was allowed to go free because the evidence against him was indirect.	
The law is not as powerful as it might appear to be and can easily be deceived.	
Blackmail is highly dangerous and can end in the blackmailer's death.	

Prewriting
Positive and Natural Law

Nobody sits down and cranks out an essay from beginning to end. Trying to do so results in a poorly organized, confusing structure. ***Prewriting*** enables the writer to do three important things: generate ideas, refine the thesis statement, and find a system for organizing the essay. Everyone has a particular favorite when it comes to techniques for prewriting, but we'll consider three.

FREEWRITING

What is freewriting?

The idea behind ***freewriting*** is simple: write anything that comes to mind without stopping to worry about whether it's relevant, smart, grammatical, or even spelled correctly. To the extent possible, write without stopping, letting each idea lead you to another. Don't edit, erase, or pause; just let it all out. The hope is that without your internal censor constantly assessing and rejecting whatever comes into your mind, the process will unearth some thoughts that might never have seen the light of day. Let's see what that would look like in response to a question about a pair of our readings from the previous chapter.

Sample freewriting

Doris is given the following assignment:

> Write an essay comparing Tolstoy's "God Sees the Truth, But Waits" on page 21 and Davisson's "The Corpus Delicti" on page 28. Your comparison should be based on a thesis that gives some insight about the legal processes at work in the stories.

To get started, Doris decides to do some freewriting.

Doris's Freewriting:

These two stories are definitely both about the law. They both are murders. One didn't really do it, and it was about theft and the other did do it and it was about blackmail. The one who didn't do it got punished and in the other story the killer got away. Actually in both stories the real killer got away. That's ironic. But this essay isn't supposed to be about irony. I wonder what else they have in common besides being ironic stories about justice not working correctly. In Tolstoy he got accused because all the signs pointed to him. Nobody saw him do it. Of course since he didn't do it. And I was kind of expecting that would mean he couldn't be found guilty. Innocent until proven guilty, but that's in America. This story is in Russia. Anyway I guess it shows that justice works better when you require that someone actually see the crime instead of just looking at indirect clues that give the impression of a crime. I think I learned that was called circumstantial evidence. It really went wrong in Aksanov's case or whatever his name was. But wait, in Davisson's story they refused to consider the circumstantial evidence and that's why he was able to go free, because no one actually saw him do it. So one story has an innocent man go to prison because of circumstantial evidence, and the other story has a guilty man go free when they won't consider that kind of evidence. It's like the two authors were having an argument with each other about whether circumstantial evidence should be listened to in court. They were both kind of manipulating their readers. That must be why Tolstoy tries so hard to make us like and feel sorry for his hero but Davisson does almost the opposite. I liked Aksyonov but I didn't feel anything for the Davisson guy.

By thinking and writing—some would say babbling—freely, Doris was able to reach an interesting realization about the stories, one that will serve as a working thesis statement. We're referring to it as a *working* thesis statement because she may well want to change it after she is done writing the rest of the essay.

Doris's Thesis Statement

These two stories offer opposing arguments as to whether circumstantial evidence should be allowed to convict a murderer.

Now the essay-in-process is in need of organization, and for that we can turn to another prewriting technique.

LISTS AND OUTLINES

What is a list?

This technique involves creating a ***list*** of every important point or fact that seems likely to belong in the essay. No attempt is made at this point to organize or prioritize the information.

Some writers will freewrite first and then use the results to build their list; others just begin with the list.

Doris's Listing

Both stories involve murders.

In both stories, the true killer is not convicted for his murder.

In both stories, the trial ends unjustly.

In both stories, nobody actually saw what happened.

In both stories, it seemed impossible that anyone else could have done the crime.

Although we don't know for sure until the end, Semyonich eventually reveals that Aksionov never committed any crime.

Aksionov is sent for 26 years to Siberia and eventually dies there.

Aksionov's story seems more tragic because he lost his family.

We admire Aksionov because he is able to forgive Semyonich.

We feel angry because Semyonich was able to fool the justice system so completely.

We feel guilty because when we don't see who killed the merchant we start to suspect Aksionov ourselves.

Aksionov was convicted only because he was found with the weapon and because the house was locked from the inside.

Ancona went free and married the woman of his choice.

We know that Ancona committed the crime because the story shows it.

Ancona's graphic and disgusting actions in disposing of the body show him to be callous and cruel.

Ancona went free because the court could not directly prove that there was a dead body or that he had caused Nina's death.

Ancona selfishly forms a plan to kill based only on a desire to get what he wants.

Ancona lives by lying to everyone, including his bride.

What is an outline?

The list is useful for getting all your ideas on paper. At that point, it's necessary to organize them by looking for ideas that belong together and putting them in groups with headings. Reviewing the list, Doris notices a way to divide the information in it. Obviously, the first items are all things the stories have in common, and obviously some items are about Aksionov while others are about Ancona. Then she notices that some of the items relate to showing how each injustice happened, but others are more focused on how readers are made to feel about each character. Doris's list would become an *outline* like this:

Doris's Outline

The stories share some basic similarities

_____

_____

_____

_____

_____

Tolstoy's innocent defendant was convicted

_____

_____

_____

Tolstoy makes us feel sorry for his defendant

_____

_____

_____

_____

Davisson's guilty defendant was acquitted

_____

_____

_____

Davisson makes us dislike his defendant

_____

_____

_____

After doing this work, it seems like Doris might want to modify her thesis statement slightly:

Doris's Revised Thesis Statement

By manipulating our reactions toward the main characters, these two stories debate whether circumstantial evidence should affect the outcome of a murder trial.

TASK LISTS AND SUBDIVIDING

What is a task list?

Yet another approach starts with a list of basic tasks that the writer feels are necessary steps. Once this list is created, examine each task and ask how it might be subdivided into smaller component tasks. Subdividing your ***task list*** can be very helpful in expanding the essay and discovering that your topic is richer and more complex than first thought. It helps prevent the dreaded "my paper is too short" syndrome.

Never try to make a paper longer by repeating yourself or by stretching clear sentences into bloated, convoluted monstrosities. Instead, remember this strategy of subdivision.

Let's consider another assignment, this time based on the two cases dealing with wills.

Sample Essay Assignment

Write an essay that argues the superiority of either Positive Law or Natural Law. Use the *Riggs* and *Pavlink* cases (pages 15 and 18) to build your argument, as well as other situations that you invent yourself.

After considering the assignment for a moment, we can make a task list as follows:

Student's Task List

1. Research and define Positive Law and Natural Law
2. Discuss *Riggs*
3. Discuss *Pavlink*
4. Discuss invented cases

Let's review the definitions of Positive Law and Natural Law before we go any further.

Definition of Positive Law and Natural Law

Those who believe in the philosophy of Positive Law argue that we must obey all laws exactly as they are written because a society cannot endure if people constantly modify or ignore laws just because they think they have a special situation. Those who believe in Natural Law argue that justice is something instinctively understood, and that it is wrong to follow a law that we know to be unjust.

For example, if a law condemns a man to prison for stealing bread to feed his starving family, a follower of Positive Law would insist that the law be applied because equal treatment is crucial. A follower of Natural Law might feel this punishment is against decency and that application of the law would be an injustice.

Armed with that knowledge, we might subdivide our task list as follows:

Subdivided Task List

1. Define Positive Law and Natural Law

    a. Give dictionary definitions

    b. Give examples

2. Discuss *Riggs*

    a. Present the facts

    b. Explain how Natural Law was used

    c. Show why Positive Law would have been unfair

3. Discuss *Pavlink*

    a. Present the facts

    b. Explain how Positive Law was used

    c. Explain why this was unfair

    d. Discuss what the decision should have been

4. Discuss an invented case

    a. Present the facts

    b. Explain how Positive Law would solve the problem unfairly

    c. Explain how Natural Law would solve the problem fairly

ADDITIONAL PRACTICE

1. Freewrite in response to the following question: "What arguments can you provide for the importance of observing natural law rather than positive law? In other words, give examples of situations showing how unfairness results when a law is applied without flexibility."

Example of Freewriting

Sometimes laws may seem fair and necessary, but they need special exceptions. One law that seems unfair is busting people for serving alcohol to minors. What if the server doesn't know they're minors? Or what if the kid lies about his age? I think it's not fair to hold the server responsible. The whole point of punishment is to punish people for trying to do something wrong. How can we expect people to spot fake ID's every time? But then if we made exceptions in those cases, that wouldn't work either because then everyone would pretend they didn't know the age of the people they're serving. Or even worse, they would stop asking their age or for their ID. Then they can always say they didn't know, as long as they didn't ask. So I guess the law has to look at things like how often it has happened to the same person, maybe. Another law that seems unfair is …

---

2. Convert the freewriting done in response to question 1 into a list. Do this by listing the laws that you believe must be enforced flexibly.

Example of Listing

1. It is a crime to sell alcohol to minors, regardless of whether the seller knows their age.

---

3.   Organize the laws that you listed in question 2 into at least three groups by finding suitable categories that the laws can fit into.

Example of Outline

A.   Laws intended to protect children

  1.   It is a crime to sell alcohol to minors, regardless of whether the seller knows their age.

---

4.   Make a list in response to the following prompt: *In the United States, many laws currently exist that offend the moral principles of a significant portion of the population. Discuss some of these laws and the principles that they offend.*

5.   Organize the list made in question 4 into at least three groups by finding suitable categories that the laws can fit into.

6.   Make a list in response to the following prompt: *In the United States, many laws currently exist that seem unnecessary, designed to govern parts of life that citizens ought to be able to manage themselves. Discuss some of these laws and explain why you feel they are unnecessary.*

7.   Organize the list made in question 6 into at least three groups by finding suitable categories that the laws can fit into.

Chapter

4

Essay Structure
Proximate Cause

BASIC ESSAY STRUCTURE

What is structure?

Documents without ***structure*** are difficult to read. Some kinds of documents have very rigid, pre-defined structures, while others are more adaptable. A college essay is somewhat flexible in structure, but the following suggestions will give a good idea of a structure to use.

Writing paragraph 1 (the introduction)

Formula for Paragraph 1

Background + Thesis Sentence

(including Roadmap that mentions Points X, Y, and Z)

For your ***Introduction***, give a few general remarks related to your topic, establishing a background that introduces the reader to the world of your subject area and shows why your topic should matter and be of interest. This background should build up or lead to your thesis sentence. Ideally, that thesis sentence will not only make a specific, provable claim about your topic, (see page 1), but will also set out a roadmap, an agenda of items that the paper will cover along the way toward proving the thesis (see page 10). While there are no magic numbers indicating how many elements should be in the roadmap, we'll assume for simplicity that there are three tasks to accomplish as part of proving the thesis. We'll call them Points X, Y, and Z.

Some professors are adamant that the thesis consist of a single sentence. If your roadmap and/or your claim are complex, that could be quite a lengthy sentence, perhaps impossibly so. It may be acceptable to set the roadmap in a sentence (or two) following the thesis sentence, but you should check with your instructor's expectations on this matter. In any event, it's probably always a good idea to have the thesis and its roadmap at the end of your first paragraph.

Writing paragraphs 2—? (the body paragraphs)

Formula for Paragraphs 2—?

Topic Sentence mentioning Point X + evidence for Point X

With the introduction out of the way, the second paragraph functions as your first **Body Paragraph**. It's a very good idea to let the first sentence always serve as a **topic sentence**, which means that it should do two things: 1) reflect the main idea of the paragraph (Point X), and 2) relate directly back to the roadmap of your thesis. If you can't easily explain how your topic sentence is one part of your overall thesis, your paragraph is destined for problems.

By the same token, you need to be able to defend the following sentences of your paragraph by showing how each and every one is a piece of proof that helps sustain the topic sentence. Sentences that can't comply with this demand for proof must be modified or eliminated.

Try to write your paragraph according to a Claim-Support-Support pattern. This means that after writing the topic sentence, you will make your first claim that supports the topic sentence. Then, before moving right away to your second claim, you elaborate on the first claim with proof, details, or reflections of that first claim. Only then do you move on to the next claim and repeat the process. Failure to do this leads to a rushed feel and claims thrown at the reader with no explanation or proof. Your essay will end up underdeveloped and too brief.

A basic essay will have one body paragraph for each point mentioned in the road map, and each body paragraph will follow the procedures discussed in this section. Note that longer, more complex essays might need several body paragraphs for each point of the road map.

Writing the last paragraph (conclusion)

Formula for Last Paragraph (Conclusion)

A last look at the subject, perhaps from a different point of view + the bottom line

---

The ***Conclusion*** prevents your essay from sounding like it has ended in mid-thought. It gives the reader an idea of how you have benefited from writing the essay and what you would like them to take from the experience. Material that may not have been directly relevant to proving your thesis can appear here as you talk a bit about how your findings apply to the world outside your essay and subject area or express an opinion about matters that your essay had treated objectively. Many writers merely recap what they had said in their introduction, but if you do this you should at least consider adding something new to avoid making this paragraph look like a pasted copy of the introduction.

Overall essay structure

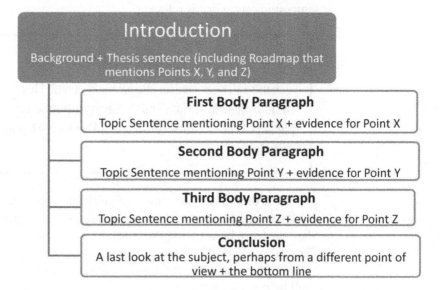

TRANSITIONS

The various components of an essay's structure will not be seen as working together unless they are connected with appropriate transitions. Transitions help to connect one paragraph to the next, but also to connect the parts of a paragraph with each other. Although in our own minds it is clear how each thought is related to the next, our readers need help in following this trail. Transitional words are like signposts that indicate these connections. They should be used generously; without them, writing appears choppy and perhaps even random. Students sometimes use inappropriate transitional words, so consider the following table for guidance.

Words of continuation

Also, Furthermore, Additionally, As well, Secondly

Purpose: Show that the current idea is finished; a new, related idea is about to be presented.

If you fail to use one of these transitional words, your reader may think you are talking about the earlier idea and be confused as to how the upcoming sentence is relevant.

Example

"Tenants can be evicted for late payment of rent. This rule exists because of the inconvenience to landlords in having to pursue payment. Such a pursuit can be very time-consuming. **(Also,)** Some tenants violate the rules of the lease."

Without the "**Also,**" a reader might think at first that violating the rules of the lease has to do with pursuing payment. Perhaps the tenant will violate the lease by shooting the landlord who is pursuing payment? In reality, tenants who violate rules turn out to be a whole separate class of people to be evicted, unrelated to the late payers. Including the "**Also**" will help make that clear.

Words of contrast

> ### But, However, On the other hand, In contrast, Then again, Yet
>
> Indicate that you are about to present an opposing idea or view.

If you fail to use one of these transitional words, your reader may think you are giving further evidence for the same argument and be confused when the evidence turns out to work against you.

> ### Example
>
> "Tenants should not be evicted when their rent is late by only one day. This kind of late payment cannot hurt the landlord significantly. (**However**,) The written contract gives the landlord this power."

Without the "**However**," a reader might think at first that the power given to the landlord is another reason for not evicting the tenant, which makes no sense. The reader may even doubt the writer's sanity. In reality, the writer was trying to give an opposing argument. Marking that with "**However**" is crucial.

Words of causation

> ### Therefore, Thus, As a result, Consequently
>
> Show that the concept just discussed is the cause of the concept about to be discussed.

If you fail to use one of these transitional words, your reader may think that your upcoming idea is just a coincidence and not see that it is caused by the concept you have just finished presenting.

> ## Example
>
> "The apartment is filled with mold. The heat does not work. **(Consequently,)** The tenants have not paid their rent for three months."

Without the "**Consequently,**" the meaning here changes drastically. A reader might think that all three conditions are happening independently, and this is just a list of all the problems going on in the building which includes tenants randomly deciding not to pay their rent. In reality, the non-payment of rent is not an independent problem but a response to the other two problems. Marking that with "**Consequently**" is crucial to the message that the reader will get here.

Words of specification

> ### For example, For instance, Specifically, In particular
>
> Show that the upcoming sentence is a specific example that illustrates the idea you have just stated.

If you fail to use one of these transitional words, your reader may think you have suddenly changed the subject for no reason.

> ## Example
>
> The rental contract contains a number of guarantees. The landlord promises that he is the true owner of the building. He promises that he will keep the building habitable. **(For example,)** He will make sure there are no problems with the appliances.

Without the "**For example,**" a reader might think that there are three separate guarantees and might be left wondering what the "habitability" promise entails. In fact, there are only two guarantees listed here. The mention of the appliances is an example of the habitability guarantee, not an additional guarantee. Leading with "**For example**" will help make that clear.

Critiquing a student's use of transitions

The following writing was done without regard to the use of transitions. Supply appropriate transitions in the blanks to help the logic and flow of the paragraph.

Sammy's conduct toward his son yesterday afternoon was extremely negligent. He had given him a gun to play with. It turns out that this gun was loaded. _____, Sammy was not watching anything that his son was doing. On several occasions, a disaster could have resulted. _____, the boy had put the gun in his mouth. _____, the boy had pointed it at his baby sister. _____, the safety mechanism of the gun was in place. Assuming it worked, this meant there was no real danger. _____, it turns out that somebody did get hurt. The boy was running around with his eyes closed. _____, he tripped, fell, and dropped the gun on his baby sister's head. _____, we spent the whole night at the emergency room. _____, the gun was damaged.

A WRITING TASK: LEGAL CAUSE

Let's apply everything we have said about essay structure to a writing assignment. You have received the following instructions:

Assignment Memo

Our client, Mr. Thief, is being charged with murder even though he never killed anybody. Admittedly, he and his friend, Mr. Buddy, did lure an intoxicated man named Victim into their truck after deliberately getting him as drunk as possible. And yes, they did drive off with him and then beat him up and take all his money … and his glasses … and some of his clothes. But they left him on the side of the highway afterward in almost perfect condition, just a little drunk and disoriented. An entire thirty minutes later, a car driven by one of those crazy college kids came hurtling down the highway and slammed right into Victim, killing him instantly.

The state now wants to charge Mr. Thief with murder, blaming him for Victim's death at the hands of the college student, Mr. Student. They are claiming that since Mr. Thief caused Victim to be on the roadside at that time, he should bear the guilt for everything that happened to him afterward.

We must fight against this injustice. I want you to prepare an argument showing that Mr. Thief cannot be designated as the legal cause of Victim's death. Afterward, I want you to prepare an argument for the opposing side so we will have an idea of what we are fighting against. To do this, you'll need to use the legal terms, "intervening cause" and "superseding cause." Don't worry, I looked them up for you.

Legal Definitions

Intervening cause—When somebody causes harm to someone else while operating with a guilty mind, the law typically punishes them. However, sometimes other events occur after the harmful action but before the harmful result. These are intervening causes. For example, if I decide I want to harass my sister by leaving her car keys in the door of her car, I am performing a harmful act. If the car gets stolen, that will be the harmful result. The thief who steals the car will be acting after my harmful act and before the result, which makes him an intervening cause.

Superseding cause—A superseding cause is an intervening cause that is so unexpected that it renders the original wrongdoer no longer legally responsible for the eventual results. In the example provided, is the thief's stealing of the car an unexpected act? Is it an act so unexpected that I should no longer be held responsible even though I'm the one who deliberately left the keys in the car door? Normally, a thief stealing a car would not be expected, but when someone deliberately leaves the keys in the car door, that probably changes the answer. So, in this case, the thief would NOT be a superseding cause and I'd be in trouble.

On the other hand, if instead of leaving those car keys in the door I just locked them in the glove compartment, out of sight, that might be a different story. Now, if a thief breaks in randomly, finds the keys, and steals the car, I might have better luck saying that I had no idea that would happen and labeling the thief a superseding cause. That would be good news for me, as it would "break the chain" of blame that was leading to me.

Deciding between Intervening and Superseding. So how do we decide when an event is a superseding cause and when it is only an intervening cause? There is no simple rule. The question to ask is, "how foreseeable was this event?" If the event was highly foreseeable or, in other words, highly expected or almost inevitable to follow the harmful act, then it will not be superseding. The original wrongdoer will remain liable. My leaving the car keys in the door all but guaranteed that someone would steal it, so the thief's act does not supersede or cancel my responsibility. On the other hand, if the event was improbable and unexpected—such as the keys stolen from the glove compartment—it is superseding. I, the original wrongdoer, may escape blame.

Generally, the more connected the intervening event is to the original wrong, the more unforeseeable it will have to be to raise it to the level of superseding. If the intervening act is a complete coincidence, we will consider it superseding if we simply hadn't foreseen it. But if we are dealing with something that is triggered quite directly by the original act, it will have to be bizarre indeed to qualify as superseding. Leaving the car keys in the door while the car is parked in a private garage on the very day when a thief happens to break into the garage is coincidental. I might have a chance after all of showing that this was unforeseeable and avoiding the blame. But if I did this while the car was parked on the street in a high-crime area, the theft is all but directly triggered by what I did. I'll need something much more bizarre than a car thief in this situation to avoid the blame.

Note on defining terms (the structure of definition)

Quite often, you'll be called upon to define terms in the course of an essay. You may even be assigned an essay with the specific purpose of defining a complex term. But don't turn to the dictionary and repeat what it says. Professors despise that. They want to hear about the subtle varieties of meaning that make defining the term a challenge, not a prewritten blurb. Here are some tips on how to write an effective definition:

- *Compare* the term to similar terms and stress what sets it apart from them.
- Write about the term's *function:* how it works or what it does.
- Identify the term's *structure:* what it's made of or how it's organized.
- Explain *where it came from* and/or how it has developed.
- Explain what the term is *not*.
- Show how the term *interacts* with other items or concepts.
- Give *examples* to illustrate the term.

Which of the techniques listed is used in the definitions you were given of intervening and superseding cause? The terms were *compared* with each other to help show their differences and show how they *interact* with each other. We saw how they *function* to assign blame. Most importantly, the *examples* helped us to understand.

Note on biased language

Biased language can be used effectively to steer the feelings and beliefs of the reader. But used unintentionally, bias can be a weakness in writing, a sign that the writer is not capable of maintaining a neutral stance. Boss's description of the case may not be a problem considering that his intended audience is one of his own employees. It would be rather inappropriate, however, in a supposedly objective newspaper article or in a report that was not supposed to take sides. Some of the bias here occurs in individual word choices while other bias comes from the way Boss has ordered and connected the facts. Where do you see evidence of bias in the Assignment Memo?

Facts of the Case: *Thief v. Victim*

based on *Kibbe v. Henderson*, 534 F.2d 493 (2nd Cir. 1976)

United States Court of Appeals, Second Circuit, 1976

Thief and his friend Buddy met Victim at a bar on an evening when Victim had been drinking heavily. Witnesses later revealed that Victim was so drunk that the bartender had refused to serve him further drinks. Thief and Buddy encouraged Victim to drink even more heavily and eventually offered him a ride. While Buddy drove, Thief robbed Victim of his money and made him lower his pants and remove his boots to prove that he had surrendered all of it. They beat him with their fists and left him on the side of a highway and drove away, leaving his boots and jacket behind as well, but not his eyeglasses. The night was freezing cold and clear. The highway had no street lighting, and the area was rural, but there was an open service station a quarter of a mile away.

Thirty minutes later, Student, a college student, was driving 50 miles per hour, which was ten miles per hour above the posted speed limit. Momentarily distracted by a flashing light on the side of the road, Student took his eyes off the road for a split second. When his eyes returned to the road, he saw Victim in the roadway, so close that he had no time to react. He collided with Victim, causing fatal injuries. The coroner determined that the beating Victim had received was superficial and that the death was completely the result of the car collision. Victim's pants were still down around his ankles at the time of his death.

Records also showed that Student's car was six months past due for a brake inspection but that the brakes had never shown any signs of problem before the night of Victim's death. Nevertheless, analysts determined that the brakes might have stopped the car in time had they been better maintained. Other witnesses revealed that Victim did not know how to read but were unable when questioned to say whether this was a result of a deeper mental impairment.

Prewriting on *Thief v. Victim*

Let's see how we would complete the first half of this assignment. Afterward, it will be up to you to write the second half.

We'll begin by constructing a task list (see page 41). We have been asked for arguments for both sides, so our task list will originally be simply this:

Task List for *Thief v. Victim*

1. Define and explain the legal terms that apply to the situation.

2. Argue that Thief is not guilty.

3. Argue that Thief is guilty.

The more we can subdivide our list before we start writing the draft, the better off we'll be. We were told to use certain legal terms. Also, common sense tells us that part of saying that Thief is not guilty should involve saying that someone else is. So we may subdivide as follows:

Revised Task List for *Thief v. Victim*

1. Define and explain the legal terms that apply to the situation.

    a. Explain that Thief definitely was one cause of Victim's death.

    b. Explain that superseding causes sometimes cancel a wrongdoer's liability for his actions.

2. Argue that Thief is not guilty.

    a. Explain why Thief's actions did not make Victim's death foreseeable.

    b. Explain why Student's actions were unforeseeable or bizarre.

3. Argue that Thief is guilty.

    a. Explain why Thief's actions did make Victim's death foreseeable.

    b. Explain why Student's actions were not unforeseeable or bizarre.

Constructing the first body paragraph

Often, it's easiest to save the first paragraph, the introduction, for last. That's because it contains the roadmap, and how can we tell the reader where we're going if we haven't gone there yet ourselves? So we start instead with the first body paragraph, which is typically the second paragraph of the essay. The task list suggests a topic sentence that introduces the concept of "superseding cause," followed by explanatory examples.

First Body Paragraph

Obviously, Victim would not have died if not for Thief's actions, but superseding causes may lead to Thief escaping legal responsibility for what happened. To understand the concept of superseding causes, we must realize that everything that happens has an infinite number of causes. Imagine that a man is run over by a bus because the driver falls unconscious due to pills that had been negligently prescribed to him. So the prescriber is a cause, but the bus driver's failure to research the pills can also be considered a cause. We call it an intervening cause because it occurred between the prescriber's wrongful act and the collision. If we decide that what the driver did was unforeseeable, we will also label his act a superseding cause, which means that it would make the prescriber no longer liable for the consequences. But, in reality, the driver's failure to research his prescribed medication seems fairly foreseeable and ordinary. That means it's only an intervening cause, not a superseding cause, and the prescriber will still be liable. To decide Thief's guilt, we need to decide whether Student's actions are superseding.

Constructing the second body paragraph

With that done, it's time to portray Thief as innocent by explaining why his actions did not make Victim's death foreseeable. The most logical approach is to consider his actions one at a time. But let's not forget first to signal what we're doing in the topic sentence. Then we'll take a claim-support-support approach where each claim will be one of Thief's actions, followed by support in the form of our thoughts as to why that action didn't lead to a foreseeable death.

1. Topic sentence is central idea of paragraph.
2. Highlighted sentences are claims, each supported by following details.
3. Bolded words are transitional words (page 52) used to signal new claims.

Second Body Paragraph

In this case, nobody could have foreseen that Thief's actions would lead to Victim's death.[1] Thief left Victim less than 30 yards from a well-lit, attended gas station.[2] This is much different from dumping him on an abandoned, dark, high-speed road. He had every reason to expect someone would notice and come to help Victim. **Further,**[3] Thief did not severely injure Victim. Although he was bleeding from his nose, there is no sign that his vision or ability to think were impaired. Someone with serious injuries might have acted desperately, but there was no reason for someone in Victim's condition to act in a way that was so hazardous for his own safety. **On the other hand,** Student's behavior was extremely unforeseeable and extraordinary. Student was driving 50 mph in a 40-mph zone. Speeding violates the law made to guarantee the safety of pedestrians. Student's speed was 25% over the limit, much more than a slight excess. Student **also** contributed to the accident by taking his eyes off the road. This is something everyone is taught never to do. When Thief left Victim on the side of the road, it would be completely unreasonable to expect that he should know there was a danger someone would take his eyes off the road and run over Victim. Such a superseding cause cancels Thief's liability.

THE STRUCTURE OF COMPARISON AND CONTRAST

Comparing two cases

Now imagine that Thief is found guilty. After going to the prison library to work on his appeal, he finds the case of *State v. Preslar* and thinks it proves that the judge made a mistake in his case. Like his own situation, the *Preslar* case involves the victim of a beating who is exposed to the cold outdoors and ends up dead.

State v. Preslar

Supreme Court of North Carolina
48 N.C. 421 (1856)

Mrs. Preslar was beaten by her husband while within their shared home, and she escaped by running into the cold winter night to seek shelter at her parents' house*. When she arrived at their home, however, she decided against waking them and instead chose to spend the night on their front porch. She died as a result of her exposure to the cold air. Preslar, her husband, was found not guilty of her murder as the night spent outdoors is labeled a superseding cause.

*Without reading further, how many parents did Ms. Preslar have? See the rules on apostrophes (page 166) to find out.

Thief is thrilled, believing that his trial judge should have followed the reasoning in the *Preslar* case. He writes a letter to his attorney, who takes one look at Thief's findings and tosses the letter on your desk.

Assignment Memo

Please look over the *Preslar* case and then write to Thief and explain to him why that situation is nothing like his.

What is a comparison/contrast?

When an assignment calls for a ***comparison / contrast,*** it is important to do more than just simply list similarities and differences at random. The comparison still has to be done for a purpose, or in other words, to prove a thesis. The reader needs to learn something about the topics other than the mere fact that there are similarities and differences between them. However, we often won't know what's interesting about the similarities and differences until we've done some prewriting about them.

One good tip, though, is that if your topics already seem fairly similar, you should concentrate your energies on detecting the differences. Conversely, if they seem to have nothing in common, it's your job to find things they share. Why? Working in the other direction would be too easy and unlikely to produce an interesting result. What's the point in arguing that a parking meter and your uncle's second-grade teacher have many differences (one is skinny while the other is fat; one is metal while the other is flesh)? If you could find a similarity, that would truly be interesting.

Organizing the comparison/contrast

Once you've listed your similarities and differences, another question is how to organize them. You have two **topics**—in this situation the *Thief* case and the *Preslar* case. And for each case, you'll want to discuss several different ways in which they differ. We'll call those the **points.** There are two strategies to organize all this information.

   Block method. The idea here is to talk exhaustively about the first topic and then to talk exhaustively about the second topic. Of course, you'll want to hit the same points in the same order on each topic.

Topic 1: Thief

    Point 1: _____

    Point 2: _____

    Point 3: _____

Topic 2: Preslar

    Point 1: _____

    Point 2: _____

    Point 3: _____

ADVANTAGE: The reader gets a clear picture of each topic without interruptions from the other topic.

DISADVANTAGE: By the time the reader reaches the second topic, the details of the first topic may be forgotten. In that case, the comparison won't be very effective.

Point-by-point method. With this scheme, discuss the first point thoroughly by considering it in relation to both topics. Then go on to the second point and do the same, etc.

```
┌─────────────────────────────────────────────────────┐
│                                                       │
│   Point 1: _____   │
│                                                       │
│     Thief: _____   │
│                                                       │
│     Preslar: _____    │
│                                                       │
│   Point 2: _____   │
│                                                       │
│     Thief: _____   │
│                                                       │
│     Preslar: _____    │
│                                                       │
│   Point 3: _____   │
│                                                       │
│     Thief: _____   │
│                                                       │
│     Preslar: _____    │
│                                                       │
└─────────────────────────────────────────────────────┘
```

ADVANTAGE: The exact differences are very clear since the reader is seeing each topic "back-to-back" with the other.

DISADVANTAGE: The constant switching back and forth between topics can be confusing or at least annoying for the reader. It may make it impossible to see the big picture of either topic.

Thinking the cases through, you realize that they look similar at first but have some very important differences. The similarity is simply that both involve a criminal doing something bad to a victim who then suffers injuries even worse than what the criminal intended. Studying more closely, we could decide that the differences lie in the following areas: 1) differences in how helpless a condition the victims were left in; 2) differences in where the victims were left; and 3) differences in how unpredictable the intervening harmful act was. Using the diagrams provided, fill in these three points to see how the plan for this essay would look.

THE STRUCTURE OF NARRATIVE
What is a narrative?

The goal of a ***narrative*** is to make the reader see clearly the details of what happened and the sequence of events. Narratives go wrong when the reader cannot picture what is being described or when the actions are jumbled together in such a way that it's impossible to tell who did what to whom, and when, where, or why it was done.

Tips for a better narrative

- Pick a point of view and stick with it. If you are describing a mugging from the victim's point of view, don't start writing about what the mugger was thinking or where he came from. If you tell your story in the past tense, stay in the past. If you tell it in the present, stay in the present. Mixing tenses confuses the reader. Don't write, "I'm walking down the street, and I turned around a corner."

- Use detail. Though it's theoretically possible to overdo it, most students need far more detail than they think. Don't write that the mugger was aggressive. Describe all his words and actions. Avoid words like "things," and "everything," if it is possible to specify what those "things" are.

- Make sequence clear. Nothing is worse than hearing a story out of order. Go from start to finish, and make it clear when things are simultaneous or when one action is triggered by another. Don't write, "The mugger smashed me over the head with a tennis racket. He had gotten the racket out of my bag that he took from me. Then he threatened me. I was very disoriented."

- Use dialogue where it matters. Hearing that the mugger made a threat is not as informative as learning that the mugger said, "If you don't give me $5, I will throw myself under a train."

Assignment Memo

Our client has offered the following narrative as part of his request for a restraining order. It needs a lot of help. Where and how would you rewrite? What would you need to ask the client to clarify? Write a letter to the client identifying the problems with the narrative and giving concrete suggestions and examples for how to improve it.

Narrative of a Request for Restraining Order

I am requesting a restraining order against my wife because of her recent behavior toward me. She has been acting crazy. On top of all that, I think my life is in danger because she has been saying things about how I will get hurt. It all began on Dec 14 when we had a fight about the telephone. That's when she throws a glass. She yells and throws things all the time. We were fighting about how on Dec 12 she had said some things that made me mad. I was going to call the police on that day, but I didn't because she talked me out of it. So after she threw the glass she made it sound like she was prepared to take it to another level. She also got our kid involved. She was screaming throughout this entire time, even before the fight about the telephone. At this point, she smashed everything in the room. I was worried about what had happened last time she did this. I was able to calm her down. She threw a glass at me when I was looking the other way. She needed to get out of my house.

Assignment Memo

Ever since Mr. Thief almost escaped his murder conviction by arguing that there was a superseding cause in his case, the local newspaper has received many angry phone calls complaining that the whole idea of superseding cause is ridiculous and should be abolished. I want to educate the public on this issue by writing an article in response, explaining why it would be unfair if courts never looked for superseding causes when a crime is committed.

I need everyone to contribute, so please write a well-developed paragraph depicting one or more situations showing how a person could receive an undeserved punishment if the superseding cause theory is ignored. In the situation you create, you'll need the following elements:

- An individual who does some kind of mild misdeed, not a completely innocent person.

- A superseding cause that results in the mild misdeed having much worse consequences than anticipated.
- Overall, a situation where it's not fair that the individual be blamed for the more severe consequences.

After creating your narrative, exchange with another student. Can you clearly visualize all the events of the story? Did the writer convince you that the superseding cause was substantial enough to clear the original criminal of legal blame?

5 Grammatical Errors
Wills · Contracts

AN UNGRAMMATICAL WILL

Why grammar matters

Let's face it. Grammar is so uninteresting to many people that it has acquired the status of a joke. A popular stereotype assumes that English professors delight in correcting other people's mistakes only to promote their own superiority. But legal experts know that an insensitivity to grammar can vastly change the meaning of a sentence, sending millions of dollars in the wrong direction, making the difference in a criminal case, and deciding the rights and responsibilities that parties owe one another. Just consider the following ordinary sentences and how their meaning can be completely inverted by changing the punctuation but not touching a single word:

> You make me the happiest. When you're not around, I'm sad. I've known you so long.

> You make me happiest when you're not around. I'm sad I've known you so long.

Imagine, then, the chaos that could be unleashed in a contract or, as we'll see here, in a will. Let's consider the scenario of a will so poorly written that it is in real danger of being executed in a matter completely contrary to its maker's wishes. Then, we'll arm ourselves with a few grammatical terms so that we can analyze and improve the will's language.

The Last Will of Edgar Doe

Assignment Memo

Our client, Edgar Doe, has recently died and left behind the most poorly written will I have ever seen. The man obviously never heard of a fragment or a run-on. I don't even know if the will is clear enough to stand up in court. Please read through the will and see if the following questions can be answered definitively. The will might be so unclear that some of these questions can't be answered.

For your information, Edgar had a brother, Rick, who is now dead. His only other brother, Todd, is not contesting anything about the will. He has one sister, Susan, who is unmarried.

Questions

1. Who gets nothing: Bob, Alice, Jane, or all three?
2. Do Rick's children get the Mercedes, the Toyota, both, or neither?
3. What does Lisa get?
4. What happens with the house in Texas?
5. What should Lisa do regarding the house in Texas?
6. What should Doe's savings be used for regarding the house in Texas?
7. What happens to Todd and to Susan?

Edgar Doe's Will

I, Edgar Doe, being of sound mind and body do hereby declare this to be my last will and testament. I want to make one thing very clear, to my son Bobby, I leave nothing to my daughters Alice and Jane I love them very much. My brother Rick's children will get my Mercedes. Unless Rick is dead. Rick's children will get my Toyota. After all my debts have been paid. The money that remains in my savings account is for my sister Lisa.

I want my house in Texas to be sold. The appliances there need to be removed before the house is listed with a prominent real estate agent. Lisa should make arrangements for the cleaning supplies and give $100 to the maid.

> I expect Todd might contest some of these decisions that will result in him being denied any money and he should not be allowed to communicate with my children. I do not want Susan to continue living in my Alaska home if she is unmarried at the time of my death she can have $3,000.

INDEPENDENT AND DEPENDENT CLAUSES

What is a clause?

A *clause* is a group of words containing a verb (action word) and a subject (the person or thing performing that action).

Laws discourage criminals from taking action.	This is a clause (Subject = Laws; Verb = discourage)
Prevented thousands of crimes.	This is not a clause. The "crimes" can't be paired with "prevented" because the crimes didn't prevent anything. Something else prevented the crimes, and since we don't know what that is, we don't have a clause.
Because they want to prevent still more crimes.	This is a clause (S = they; V = want)
Lawmakers who just want to help.	This is not a clause. The subject is "Lawmakers," but "want" only tells us which lawmakers we're talking about. We still don't know what these lawmakers do.
Lawmakers who just want to help often try too hard.	This is a clause. (S = lawmakers; V = try).

What is the difference between an independent clause and a dependent clause?

When a clause has enough information that it makes sense by itself, we call it an *independent clause*—independent because it doesn't need any other words to qualify as an English sentence. When a clause leaves the reader requiring more words before it can make sense, we call it a *dependent clause.*

Lawmakers try to stop crimes before they happen.	Independent Clause
Lawmakers write bills.	Independent Clause
Because they have training.	Dependent Clause
When a majority of the voters elect a candidate to office.	Dependent Clause
Lawmakers who just want to help often try too hard.	Independent Clause

Some students have trouble distinguishing the two, thinking that if an expression leaves any unanswered questions, it must be a dependent clause. That's not the right way to think about it. It's not reasonable to expect that any one sentence is going to contain all the answers. So, for example, "He passed that bill last December" is an independent clause. It leaves the reader wondering who "he" is and which bill is "that bill," but it still makes sense in a way that merely writing "that bill last December" or "passed that bill last December" does not. Here are two tests to help you tell an independent clause from a dependent clause.

The Telephone Test

To decide if a certain expression is a dependent clause, imagine a phone conversation in which your caller starts the conversation by just stating that expression. Would you think the caller was crazy? Again, the test is not whether you would know exactly what was being talked about but whether you would think the caller was totally deranged.

Lawmakers have gone too far.	Independent clause. This makes sense. You don't know what they did, but it makes sense. You'd ask your caller why they are angry with the lawmakers.
Who have gone too far.	Dependent clause. You would conclude that your caller is out of his mind and hang up.
The woman in charge of the committee broke her deal with him.	Independent clause. This makes sense even though you would need to ask which committee or what deal or with whom.
After the woman in charge of the committee.	Dependent clause. You would have no idea even what to ask and would instead hang up.

The Make-It-A-Question Test

See if you can turn the word-group into a question. If you can, it's probably an independent clause. If not, that's a clue that it makes no sense by itself and is a dependent clause.

Lawmakers have gone too far.	Have lawmakers gone too far? (It's a independent clause)
Have gone too far.	**NO QUESTION POSSIBLE** (It's a dependent clause)
The woman in charge of the committee broke her deal with him.	Has the woman in charge of the committee broken her deal with him? (It's an independent clause)
The woman in charge of the committee.	**NO QUESTION POSSIBLE** (It's a dependent clause)

FRAGMENTS

What is a fragment?

Now that we are familiar with independent and dependent clauses, ***fragments*** are easy to discuss. A fragment is an expression that is too incomplete to be considered a full sentence. Sometimes this might be a group of words that obviously lacks something essential, such as a subject or verb.

Examples of Fragments

Especially prisoners. The correctional officers with more experience. Beating the inmates. Deprive them of basic rights that the Constitution guarantees.

These are all fragments, and as you can see, the length of an expression is no guarantee it won't be a fragment. You might think it impossible that anyone would try to pass one of those off as a sentence, but it happens frequently when a writer sets down a full sentence and then wants to set down an afterthought but forgets that the afterthought cannot stand alone, "pretending" to be a full sentence. The following passage gives a better idea of how fragments can sneak in.

More Fragments

People out of the workforce have a difficult time reentering. Especially prisoners. The prison sends different officers to work with them. The correctional officers with more experience. Sometimes they exceed their authority. Beating the inmates. They feel it is acceptable to abuse them. Deprive them of basic rights that the Constitution guarantees.

Sometimes students overlook a fragment because they see a subject and verb and think it must be a complete sentence. But, as we just saw, that's not necessarily so. If the expression is a dependent clause, it will have a subject and verb but still not be a sentence. Here are some examples:

- When some prisoners try to educate themselves.
- Because they have better opportunities.
- After the guards beat the inmates.
- If prisoners are deprived of basic rights.

Repairing fragments

Remembering that dependent clauses earned their name by needing more words to communicate a full idea, we can see that the way to fix these is to add more words answering the question that leaves the reader dangling. What happens when prisoners try to educate themselves? What happens because they have more experience? What happens after beating the inmates? What happens if prisoners are deprived of basic rights? Try repairing each of the fragments by adding extra words before or after.

A second way to fix these is just to erase the word that makes them dependent clauses, which in each case is the very first word. Once those words are gone, the clauses become independent clauses.

- Some prisoners try to educate themselves.
- They have better opportunities.
- The guards beat the inmates.
- Prisoners are deprived of basic rights.

RUN-ONS

What is a run-on?

If a fragment occurs when an expression is missing something, ***run-ons*** occur when an expression takes on too much. Contrary to what many think, a run-on can't be defined as a sentence that is too long, though. Instead, a run-on occurs when two or more independent clauses have been put together in a single expression without being correctly joined.

A Run-on

Prisoners try to educate themselves, they have nothing else to do.

Here, the part before the comma is an independent clause, but so is the part after the comma. Remember that even though readers, without more information, may not know who "they" are, the word "they" still acts as a subject. The clause still makes sense. The problem then is that these two independent clauses have been placed back-to-back rather than properly joined. A comma by itself is never a proper way to join independent clauses. In fact, a run-on that results from an attempt to join independent clauses with only a comma occurs so frequently that the error has its own name—the ***comma splice***.

How to repair a run-on

One solution for dealing with a run-on is simply to split it up. This can be done with either a period or a semi-colon (;). The semi-colon is a very infrequently used punctuation mark that can be used whenever, and only whenever, a period is appropriate. It implies that the two sentences on either side are closely related to each other. If this sounds a little difficult to judge, it is. For this reason, learning writers should just avoid the semi-colon altogether and use periods.

A second solution is to connect the two independent clauses with an appropriate conjunction **together with a comma.** The comma alone is not enough. Appropriate conjunctions are easy to remember as there are only seven and they all are three letters or less: *For, And, Nor, But, Or, Yet,* and *So.* Their initial letters spell FANBOYS.

The third solution is to change one of the independent clauses so that it becomes a dependent clause. All this takes generally is adding a ***subordinating*** word to the beginning of the clause so that it no longer makes sense by itself. Typical subordinating words include *After, Before, When, Because, If,* and *Although*. They are called "subordinate" because the idea they introduce is secondary to the rest of the sentence. In the sentence "Prisoners face problems after they leave" the words in the "after they leave" clause just set the timeframe of when prisoners face problems. Thus, they are subordinate.

So our sample run-on can be fixed in three ways:

Prisoners try to educate themselves. They have nothing else to do *or* Prisoners try to educate themselves; they have nothing else to do.	Split them up with a period or semi-colon
Prisoners try to educate themselves, and they have nothing else to do.	Join them with a comma **AND** a FANBOYS word
Prisoners try to educate themselves because they have nothing else to do.	Add a subordinating word to one of the independent clauses, thereby turning it into a dependent clause

A special run-on trap

Notice, by the way, that there are some words that are frequently misused to connect two independent clauses. Words like *However, Therefore,* and *Otherwise* don't fit either of the two solutions provided. They are not part of the two- or three-letter FANBOYS "collection." Also, adding them to an independent clause doesn't make the clause any less independent. For example, changing "Prisoners are deprived of basic rights" to "However, prisoners are deprived of basic rights" doesn't stop that sentence from making perfect sense. Since these words aren't appropriate connectors, commonly found expressions such as these are run-ons:

> WRONG: Some prisoners try to educate themselves, therefore they have more experience.

> WRONG: Guards beat the prisoners, however the prisoners still have some rights.

Practice with run-ons

The web is full of sites that will allow you to practice recognizing and repairing fragments and run-ons. It is highly recommended that you practice on some of these sites by entering the terms *fragments* and *run-ons* into a search engine.

Much of the difficulty with run-ons may come from simply not believing that the issue matters. It's true that in many cases a run-on won't prevent a reader from understanding what you meant. But many run-ons together, and occasionally even a single one, can cause tremendous confusion. Look at the passage that follows and see how many confusing moments you can identify. How would you eliminate the run-ons to remove the confusion?

An Exercise with Run-ons

There were a lot of problems for the beach people were trying to escape the floodwaters rose higher than they ever had before anything can be done the mayor will have to get clearance from the president's office it can be very hard to get answers that will make the recovery process difficult and delayed mail service will also contribute to an ordeal we will never improve our response to this sort of emergency if we don't set some priorities above all other things we must remain calm.

Examining a contract with run-ons

Run-ons become particularly important when writing a legal document such as a contract. Failure to make clear which words go with which could lead to a document that says the opposite of what was intended.

Assignment Memo

I need you to read through this section of our client's contract to see if it is clear. Please do the following:

1. Read it through once and assess the impression it gave you by answering the questions beneath it.

2. Then read it again to see if it could be understood in different ways.

3. Finally, fix any run-ons to make it clearer.

The Contract

Professors will be paid at full salary during their vacation periods that are spent doing research will be reimbursed as well wherever possible such research should be documented thoroughly to avoid confusion the university will not guarantee payment for undocumented hours if a professor has a previous release form that states otherwise that release form will not be enforced unless it is signed the research documentation will be rejected.

Questions

1. Are professors guaranteed to be paid at full salary during vacation and during research, or only during vacation, or only during vacations that they spend doing research?

2. Are professors guaranteed to be paid for research or only wherever possible?

3. How does the situation change for a professor who has a previous release form?

4. What is it that has to be signed?

PARALLEL STRUCTURE

What is parallel structure?

A common problem that students face is the use of *parallel structure*, sometimes called parallelism. This principle requires that all elements of a written list, even if the list contains only two items, must be in the same grammatical form. To start with a simple example, we should write, *"State prisons are depressing, humiliating, and boring,"* not, *"State prisons are depressing, humiliate people, and boredom."*

Failure to use parallelism risks confusing the reader. If all items of the list follow the same grammatical form, it is clear that they belong together. If the items don't match, though, the reader may doubt he's drawing the proper meaning. Consider this pair:

Parallel Structure

Not Parallel: State prisoners experience humiliation, depressed, and cruel guards.

Parallel: State prisoners experience humiliation, depression, and cruel guards.

In the first version, who is depressed? It sounds more like the guards are depressed, though the reader suspects it was meant to be the prisoners. The second, parallel version removes all doubt.

Examining a will with parallel structure problems

Assignment Memo

Our client, Julio, has provided us with a draft of what he wants the first part of his will to look like. As you will see, it is terribly confusing in its lack of parallel structure. Please review his draft, detect the sources of confusion, and improve them by repairing the faulty parallelism. Be prepared to explain to the client where the confusion lay.

Julio's Will

I want my wife Alice to inherit the family home if she quits smoking, getting a new job, and gambling.

I direct that my brother should not only have custody of my children but also my horse.

Money from my trust fund should be used to recruit new salespeople in my business, increasing revenues, and refinishing the floor.

Money from my stocks should be spent for improving the house, replacing the furniture, and my brother Ben.

If both of my parents are still living, I want them to receive $500 each, have the right to use my Los Angeles home indefinitely, my Mercedes, and care for my dog, and all my plants.

I leave $1,000 to my wife, $400 to charity, and to my brothers.

I want this entire will to be canceled if I die in an odd-numbered year, before the age of 50, or I die as the result of criminal activity.

Chapter

6

Integrating Source Material
Evidence

SUPPORT

What is support?

One of the most common shortcomings in student writing is the lack of substantial, convincing support. Just as evidence is necessary in the courtroom to convict a criminal or convince a judge that one party deserves compensation, an essay requires support to convince a reader to take action, to change his or her views, or to believe that the writer has mastered the subject.

And just as in the courtroom, evidence is no good if it is not:

- Coming from a reliable, verifiable source
- Highly specific
- Clearly relevant to the case at hand
- Coming from a variety of angles
- Presented clearly and connected logically to the case

Bad use of evidence

Imagine a trial. The prosecuting attorney is pacing across the floor, building her case against Charlie the Child Endangerer. She explains that Charlie has three children, at which point she produces a photograph of five children and flings it at the jury box. She goes on to say that Charlie is often distracted by his busy work schedule, pausing to hold a laptop computer and a screwdriver in front of the jury. On June 7, she tells the jury, the children were asleep in their bed. She lays a bedsheet on the courtroom floor as she says this. All this time, she explains, the chili he was cooking was burning and emitting smoke. She drops a can of chili and a smoke detector into the jury box and turns to the judge saying "The People rest."

Why is the jury baffled? They figured out that Charlie's children are probably in the photo, but of course don't know which three they are supposed to be looking at or why it matters what they look like. They are clueless as to what the computer and screwdriver have to do with Charlie's work and what, if anything, they should notice about them. They conclude that the bedsheet is from the children's bed but can't imagine that it's necessary to see it and are similarly confused about the can and the smoke detector. Is it possible to tell that the smoke detector has gone off recently, or is it just here for decoration? And even if it has gone off recently, how do we even know it is from Charlie's house? The attorney hasn't connected the evidence to her story, hasn't guided the audience in what to see in it, and has brought in things that probably don't need to be there at all.

Make sure you don't do this in your writing. Don't fling evidence at the reader without introducing it or directing the reader's attention to the aspects that interest you. And don't quote material from a text when it would be just as effective to use your own words.

INTEGRATING QUOTES

The problem of the floating quotation

First of all, here's what to avoid doing.

Bad Integration of Quote

The husband denied ever having neglected the children. "I always cared for them 100%." The mother also says she has been responsible.

The error shown here is called a floating quotation. Instead of being connected to one of the writer's sentences, it is its own sentence. In this particular example, it's especially hard to see whether the quote belongs to the father or the mother. But even in less extreme situations, it is bad, sloppy style to let a quote float free like that.

Now, we will look at the principles of how to integrate the quote properly.

Introduce the quote

This involves putting some words before the quote that explain who is talking, from what situation the words are coming, and how this quote is related to what's going on in your essay at the moment.

Use common sense to decide how to characterize the speaker of the quote. If this is a famous person, use the full name—"Martin Luther King, Jr., has said. . . ." If the person is unknown, it is better to introduce by title or position—"Nancy Prin, a spokesperson for the Centers of Disease Control, has said. . . ." In fact, if you never plan to refer to this person by name again, you might use only the title and drop the name altogether. After introducing a speaker formally, you can just use the last name for future references (without the Mr. or Ms.), but don't ever use just a first name.

Connect the quote

There are three ways to connect the quote to the rest of your sentence. The one you choose will depend on how the lead-in to your sentence looks.

Rule	Example
If the lead-in is a full sentence, use a **colon** (:)	The father's testimony showed confusion: "I love all three or four of these kids."
If the lead-in is an incomplete thought that ends with "said" or its equivalent, use a **comma** (,)	The father testified, "I love all three or four of these kids."
If the lead-in flows directly into the quote with no obvious signs that a quote is even being inserted, this is called a **blended quote** and needs no extra punctuation marks at all.	The father's pathetic protest that he loves "all three or four of these kids" said much about his incompetence.

More about the blended quote

Students are often the least sure about this last option, but it is the most effective and deserves a little more commentary. The blended quote is effective because it allows the writer to quote without constantly interrupting the flow of the essay. A sentence can weave in and out of quotes, even including multiple quotes in the same sentence without having to use a monotonous and repetitive, *"She said this. And he said this. Then he said this."*

You may be familiar with the practice of making little quotation marks in the air with two fingers of each hand while speaking. For example, I might say that Elena is very happy with her new career. But while saying "career," I make little quotation gestures with my fingers. Why? I do it to emphasize that Elena calls it a career but that I don't personally think the word is appropriate. In other words, I think her new occupation is a joke. If I hadn't made the little quotation gestures, my sarcasm might have gone unnoticed. I did it this way because I thought it was more clever than saying, "Elena has a new job. She said, 'This is my new career,' but I don't think it deserves to be called that."

Similarly, I could mock Elena's hairstyle by asking what people thought of her new "hairstyle," implying that it is too disastrous to be considered a style. It seems the finger gestures are usually used to mock someone, and of course quotations in an essay have many more uses than that. But the idea is the same: a listener would not even detect that a quotation was occurring without seeing the quotation marks. No announcement of the quote is made the way it is with the comma and colon methods shown.

While the blended quote is the most elegant and versatile, all three methods have their place.

Practice with introducing quotes

Most of the following quotes have one or more problems with the way they are introduced. Beside each quote, indicate which problem(s) you see by listing the corresponding number:

1. Problems with punctuation

2. Reader has no idea who or what kind of person is speaking

3. The quote does not flow grammatically with the rest of the sentence

4. The quote does not seem logically related to the rest of the sentence

5. No problems

Quote	Problem(s)
I think people would accept immigrants more if they learned the language. "Every immigrant who comes here should be required within five years to learn English or leave the country."	
Dealing with immigration is one of our country's greatest challenges: "no longer the conquest of the wilderness but the absorption of fifty different peoples."	
It is unclear which aliens would be barred by this new law since it refers only to aliens who have committed "morally offensive crimes."	
Clearly the law was drafted by bigots since it actually refers to undocumented immigrants as: "intruders," "invaders," and "colonizers."	
The report showed that some immigrants have family here already: "while the vast majority of people crossing a land border are from Latin America, many are from Canada."	
We urge you to vote against amnesty. It is, "a big billboard, a flashing billboard, to the rest of the world that we don't really mean our immigration law."	
A recent editorial argues that women and men are treated differently, "Imprisoning undocumented immigrants costs us money and does not make us safer, aside from criminal cases."	
For some reason, the judge kept referring to lines from Shakespeare while giving his opinion. "The defendant must realize that what is done cannot be undone."	
I think we should remember that "and many immigrants have no family ties back in their country of origin."	
This applicant has extremely strong recommendations: "He is one of the most honest and generous people I have ever met."	

To quote or not to quote

Many students have acquired the idea that they must quote as frequently as possible in a college paper in order to get a good grade. This is only partially true at best.

The truth is that students need to refer to specific evidence as frequently as possible. That may or may not be in the form of quotations. One of the most difficult skills to acquire is a sense of when it's appropriate to quote, and when it's better to describe the material in your own words—that is, to paraphrase it.

Think again of the courtroom. Attorneys don't drag in physical versions of every single word they mention in their presentation. An impatient judge would become very angry if an attorney couldn't immediately and concisely state why a certain piece of evidence was brought in. So, too, you must be prepared to defend the existence of every quote in your paper by explaining why you felt it necessary that the reader see the exact words.

You can defend the existence of a quote in your essay on one or more of several grounds:

1. Something about the choice of words is significant, and failure to quote would prevent you from making a point about that choice of words.

    a. The words might show the speaker's tone, attitude, or state of mind, which you want to discuss.

    b. The words might be ambiguous, able to be interpreted in multiple ways. You want to explore the possible meanings.

    c. The words themselves might be more important than the meaning behind them. You are making a point about the writer's or speaker's style.

    d. The words are so incredibly eloquent that you feel it would be a real loss not to preserve them in your essay just as they are.

    e. Someone impressive said the words, and you feel your point will be more credible by dropping them into your essay.

Practice with justifying use of quotes

Let's see some examples of those. In the following table, indicate which rule you think could be used to defend the use of the quote or place an "X" if you think there is no justification for the quote.

Quote	Rule that Justifies its Use
I think people would accept immigrants more if they learned the language. Even President Theodore Roosevelt once said, "Every immigrant who comes here should be required within five years to learn English or leave the country."	
Dealing with immigration is one of our country's greatest challenges. As Walter Lippmann said, our task is "no longer the conquest of the wilderness but the absorption of fifty different peoples."	
It is unclear which aliens would be barred by this new law since it refers only to aliens who have committed "morally offensive crimes."	
Clearly the law was drafted by bigots since it actually refers to undocumented immigrants as "intruders," "invaders," and "colonizers."	
The director of the Border Patrol has said that "while the vast majority of people crossing a land border are from Latin America, many are from Canada."	
We urge you to vote against amnesty, which has been aptly described by Richard Lamm as "a big billboard, a flashing billboard, to the rest of the world that we don't really mean our immigration law."	
The law is written in such a way that requires specialized training to read: "It shall henceforth be no defense to a charge of inadmissibility that a conviction terminated in a dismissal for the interests of justice, as opposed to a dismissal based on the merits, notwithstanding any statutory relief on the state level that speaks to the matter of expungement as such relief would be preempted by federal interests."	
A recent editorial argues that it is costly and unnecessary to put undocumented immigrants in prisons if they are not criminals: "Imprisoning undocumented immigrants costs us money and does not make us safer, aside from criminal cases."	
For some reason, the judge kept referring to lines from Shakespeare while giving his opinion: "the defendant must realize that what is done cannot be undone."	
Studies show that "many immigrants have no family ties back in their country of origin."	
This applicant has extremely strong recommendations. In fact, a state governor has written in his support, "He is one of the most honest and generous people I have ever met."	
As the proceeding ended, the applicant promised, "I will stay out of all trouble and comply with all laws."	

Quote	Rule that Justifies its Use
The applicant's promise to "obey all laws that seemed fair" was not very convincing.	
We are not sure whether the applicant's promise, "I'll do what I have to do," is a good sign or not.	
The senator said that immigrants need to "integrate into society," which could be taken as racist.	
The senator's concluding words left the crowd wondering if he even knew what he was talking about: "The reforms that were passed have been okay, but we could make some changes. We need to shore things up and look at the big picture, but I think we can do it."	
The senator said that his top priorities were now "immigration and education," and that he was eager to get to work.	

Excerpting quotes

In keeping with the idea that excessive quoting can be distracting, it's often a good idea to use only part of a quote. This ensures that the reader will focus on just the part of the quote that is important and keeps your paper from being taken over by quotes. There are two useful techniques.

1. **Use blended quotes.** With blended quotes you can pluck the important parts out of your source and connect them with your own words.

Example of Blended Quotes used to Excerpt

Original: One difference between a crime and a tort is that society in its infinite wisdom strongly feels that those who perpetrate crimes should be vindictively punished by the government, whereas those who commit torts can right their wrong by contritely paying damages directly to their victims.

Quoted: The writer makes a distinction between being "vindictively punished by the government" and "contritely paying damages."

2. **Use Ellipsis.** Otherwise known as "dot dot dot," the ellipsis allows you to cut words out of the middle of a quotation. Two important warnings apply with this fun tool, however. Make sure you are not changing the meaning, such as by cutting a vital word like "not." Just as importantly, make sure that the sentence that remains still reads as a valid English sentence.

Example of Ellipsis used to Excerpt

Original: One difference between a crime and a tort is that society in its infinite wisdom strongly feels that those who perpetrate crimes should be vindictively punished by the government, whereas those who commit torts can right their wrong by contritely paying damages directly to their victims.

Quoted: As for crimes and torts, the writer claims, "One difference . . . is that . . . those who perpetrate crimes should be vindictively punished by the government, whereas those who commit torts can right their wrong by contritely paying damages directly to their victims."

Wrong: As for crimes and torts, the writer claims, "One difference between a crime and a tort is that society in its infinite wisdom strongly feels that those who perpetrate crime . . . by the government, whereas those who commit torts can . . . paying damages directly to their victims."

Practice integrating and excerpting quotes

Assignment Memo

We have been asked to respond to a complaint against Local University. The complaint alleges that the practice of allowing live bands to play in the campus quad is disruptive and asks that the practice be discontinued. We have obtained a number of letters from students, some attacking and others defending the tradition.

I would like you to prepare a response ***defending*** the practice of live bands on campus. Your response should mostly focus on introducing and critiquing the student remarks. That means discrediting and dismissing the negative comments and emphasizing the positive comments. Some of those positive comments are a little silly, too, so try to excerpt them in a way that makes them look intelligent without changing the meaning.

Please use a variety of methods for introducing the quotes (comma method, colon method, blended quote) so as to avoid monotony. Incorporate at least six quotes.

Student Remarks about Live Bands on Campus

1. "This is a college, not a mall. We don't need entertainment here, and I don't see why we're even spending money on something like this."

2. "I wouldn't mind if the bands were any good, but most of them suck. So what's the point?"

3. "Some people are just too negative. College isn't supposed to be all work. Without these bands, student morale would go down and people might even start going to different campuses that aren't so uptight."

4. "I wouldn't really know because I only come to school during the first and last week of class."

5. "What these people don't understand is that music is a form of art and stuff. We owe it to our students to provide alternate educational stuff like exposure to these bands and stuff."

6. "I had to take a test last week with some band blasting so loud that I couldn't concentrate even with the doors shut. I felt totally betrayed by my college, and I wanted to rush out there and personally destroy each member of the band."

7. "I think music is the universal language. Why would anyone not like music?"

8. "I think it's great. What if some new band, like, gets discovered here at El Camino? You have to look at the big picture."

9. "The real problem is that the selection of the bands is totally prejudiced. My friends and I tried to get our band approved to play on campus and we were totally rejected, and it was so unfair."

10. "There's one very simple word to describe the lunch-time bands, and that word is noise pollution."

WILLIAM FAULKNER'S "A ROSE FOR EMILY"

We will practice the art of gathering evidentiary support and integrating it by developing a number of different arguments about a murder that occurs in a famous short story by William Faulkner. Following the story are a number of assignments that require you to mine the story for evidence and make decisions about what will be useful as evidence, when to quote, and how to integrate any quotes.

A Rose for Emily

by William Faulkner

When Miss Emily Grierson died, our whole town went to her funeral: the men through a sort of respectful affection for a fallen monument, the women mostly out of curiosity to see the inside of her house, which no one save an old man-servant—a combined gardener and cook—had seen in at least ten years.

It was a big, squarish frame house that had once been white, decorated with cupolas and spires and scrolled balconies in the heavily lightsome style of the seventies, set on what had once been our most select street. But garages and cotton gins had encroached and obliterated even the august names of that neighborhood; only Miss Emily's house was left, lifting its stubborn and coquettish decay above the cotton wagons and the gasoline pumps—an eyesore among eyesores. And now Miss Emily had gone to join the representatives of those august names where they lay in the cedar-bemused cemetery among the ranked and anonymous graves of Union and Confederate soldiers who fell at the battle of Jefferson.

Alive, Miss Emily had been a tradition, a duty, and a care; a sort of hereditary obligation upon the town, dating from that day in 1894 when Colonel Sartoris, the mayor—he who fathered the edict that no Negro woman should appear on the streets without an apron—remitted her taxes, the dispensation dating from the death of her father on into perpetuity. Not that Miss Emily would have accepted charity. Colonel Sartoris invented an involved tale to the effect that Miss Emily's father had loaned money to the town, which the town, as a matter of business, preferred this way of repaying. Only a man of Colonel Sartoris' generation and thought could have invented it, and only a woman could have believed it.

When the next generation, with its more modern ideas, became mayors and aldermen, this arrangement created some little dissatisfaction. On the first of the year they mailed her a tax notice. February came, and there was no reply. They wrote her a formal letter, asking her to call at the sheriff's office at her convenience. A week later the mayor wrote her himself, offering to call or to send his car for her, and received in reply a note on paper of an archaic shape, in a thin, flowing calligraphy in faded ink, to the effect that she no longer went out at all. The tax notice was also enclosed, without comment.

They called a special meeting of the Board of Aldermen. A deputation waited upon her, knocked at the door through which no visitor had passed since she ceased giving china-painting lessons eight or ten years earlier. They were admitted by the old Negro into a dim hall from which a stairway mounted into still more shadow. It smelled of dust and disuse—a close, dank smell. The Negro led them into the parlor. It was furnished in heavy, leather-covered furniture. When the Negro opened the blinds of one window, they could see that the leather was cracked; and when they sat down, a faint dust rose sluggishly about their thighs, spinning with slow motes in the single sun-ray. On a tarnished gilt easel before the fireplace stood a crayon portrait of Miss Emily's father.

They rose when she entered—a small, fat woman in black, with a thin gold chain descending to her waist and vanishing into her belt, leaning on an ebony cane with a tarnished gold head. Her skeleton was small and spare; perhaps that was why what would have been merely plumpness in another was obesity in her. She looked bloated, like a body long submerged in motionless water, and of that pallid hue. Her eyes, lost in the fatty ridges of her face, looked like two small pieces of coal pressed into a lump of dough as they moved from one face to another while the visitors stated their errand.

She did not ask them to sit. She just stood in the door and listened quietly until the spokesman came to a stumbling halt. Then they could hear the invisible watch ticking at the end of the gold chain.

Her voice was dry and cold. "I have no taxes in Jefferson. Colonel Sartoris explained it to me. Perhaps one of you can gain access to the city records and satisfy yourselves."

"But we have. We are the city authorities, Miss Emily. Didn't you get a notice from the sheriff, signed by him?"

"I received a paper, yes," Miss Emily said. "Perhaps he considers himself the sheriff. . . . I have no taxes in Jefferson."

"But there is nothing on the books to show that, you see. We must go by the—"

"See Colonel Sartoris. I have no taxes in Jefferson."

"But, Miss Emily—"

"See Colonel Sartoris." (Colonel Sartoris had been dead almost ten years.) "I have no taxes in Jefferson. Tobe!" The Negro appeared. "Show these gentlemen out."

II

So she vanquished them, horse and foot, just as she had vanquished their fathers thirty years before about the smell. That was two years after her father's death and a short time after her sweetheart—the one we believed would marry her—had deserted her. After her father's death she went out very little; after her sweetheart went away, people hardly saw her at all. A few of the ladies had the temerity to call, but were not received, and the only sign of life about the place was the Negro man—a young man then—going in and out with a market basket.

"Just as if a man—any man—could keep a kitchen properly," the ladies said; so they were not surprised when the smell developed. It was another link between the gross, teeming world and the high and mighty Griersons.

A neighbor, a woman, complained to the mayor, Judge Stevens, eighty years old.

"But what will you have me do about it, madam?" he said.

"Why, send her word to stop it," the woman said. "Isn't there a law?"

"I'm sure that won't be necessary," Judge Stevens said. "It's probably just a snake or a rat that nigger of hers killed in the yard. I'll speak to him about it."

The next day he received two more complaints, one from a man who came in diffident deprecation. "We really must do something about it, Judge. I'd be the last one in the world to bother Miss Emily, but we've got to do something." That night the Board of Aldermen met—three graybeards and one younger man, a member of the rising generation.

"It's simple enough," he said. "Send her word to have her place cleaned up. Give her a certain time to do it in, and if she don't . . ."

"Dammit, sir," Judge Stevens said, "will you accuse a lady to her face of smelling bad?"

So the next night, after midnight, four men crossed Miss Emily's lawn and slunk about the house like burglars, sniffing along the base of the brickwork and at the cellar openings while one of them performed a regular sowing motion with his hand out of a sack slung from his shoulder. They broke open the cellar door and sprinkled lime there, and in all the outbuildings. As they recrossed the lawn, a window that had been dark was lighted and Miss Emily sat in it, the light behind her, and her upright torso motionless as that of an idol. They crept quietly across the lawn and into the shadow of the locusts that lined the street. After a week or two the smell went away.

That was when people had begun to feel really sorry for her. People in our town, remembering how old lady Wyatt, her great-aunt, had gone completely crazy at last, believed that the Griersons held themselves a little too high for what they really were. None of the young men were quite good enough for Miss Emily and such. We had long thought of them as a tableau; Miss Emily a slender figure in white in the background, her father a spraddled silhouette in the foreground, his back to her and clutching a horsewhip, the two of them framed by the back-flung front door. So when she got to be thirty and was still single, we were not pleased exactly, but vindicated; even with insanity in the family she wouldn't have turned down all of her chances if they had really materialized.

When her father died, it got about that the house was all that was left to her; and in a way, people were glad. At last they could pity Miss Emily. Being left alone, and a pauper, she had become humanized. Now she too would know the old thrill and the old despair of a penny more or less.

The day after his death all the ladies prepared to call at the house and offer condolence and aid, as is our custom. Miss Emily met them at the door, dressed as usual and with no trace of grief on her face. She told them that her father was not dead. She did that for three days, with the ministers calling on her, and the doctors, trying to persuade her to let them dispose of the body. Just as they were about to resort to law and force, she broke down, and they buried her father quickly.

We did not say she was crazy then. We believed she had to do that. We remembered all the young men her father had driven away, and we knew that with nothing left, she would have to cling to that which had robbed her, as people will.

III

She was sick for a long time. When we saw her again, her hair was cut short, making her look like a girl, with a vague resemblance to those angels in colored church windows—sort of tragic and serene.

The town had just let the contracts for paving the sidewalks, and in the summer after her father's death they began the work. The construction company came with niggers and mules and machinery, and a foreman named Homer Barron, a Yankee—a big, dark, ready man, with a big voice and eyes lighter than his face. The little boys would follow in groups to hear him cuss the niggers, and the niggers singing in time to the rise and fall of picks. Pretty soon he knew everybody in town. Whenever you heard a lot of laughing anywhere about the square, Homer Barron would be in the center of the group. Presently we began to see him and Miss Emily on Sunday afternoons driving in the yellow-wheeled buggy and the matched team of bays from the livery stable.

At first we were glad that Miss Emily would have an interest, because the ladies all said, "Of course a Grierson would not think seriously of a Northerner, a day laborer." But there were still others, older people, who said that even grief could not cause a real lady to forget *noblesse oblige*—without calling it *noblesse oblige*. They just said, "Poor Emily. Her kinsfolk should come to her." She had some kin in Alabama; but years ago her father had fallen out with them over the estate of old lady Wyatt, the crazy woman, and there was no communication between the two families. They had not even been represented at the funeral.

And as soon as the old people said, "Poor Emily," the whispering began. "Do you suppose it's really so?" they said to one another. "Of course it is. What else could . . ." This behind their hands; rustling of craned silk and satin behind jalousies closed upon the sun of Sunday afternoon as the thin, swift clop-clop-clop of the matched team passed: "Poor Emily."

She carried her head high enough—even when we believed that she was fallen. It was as if she demanded more than ever the recognition of her dignity as the last Grierson; as if it had wanted that touch of earthiness to reaffirm her imperviousness. Like when she bought the rat poison, the arsenic. That was over a year after they had begun to say "Poor Emily," and while the two female cousins were visiting her.

"I want some poison," she said to the druggist. She was over thirty then, still a slight woman, though thinner than usual, with cold, haughty black eyes in a face the flesh of which was strained across the temples and about the eyesockets as you imagine a light house-keeper's face ought to look. "I want some poison," she said.

"Yes, Miss Emily. What kind? For rats and such? I'd recom—"

"I want the best you have. I don't care what kind."

The druggist named several. "They'll kill anything up to an elephant. But what you want is—"

"Arsenic," Miss Emily said. "Is that a good one?"

"Is . . . arsenic? Yes, ma'am. But what you want—"

"I want arsenic."

The druggist looked down at her. She looked back at him, erect, her face like a strained flag. "Why, of course," the druggist said. "If that's what you want. But the law requires you to tell what you are going to use it for."

Miss Emily just stared at him, her head tilted back in order to look him eye for eye, until he looked away and went and got the arsenic and wrapped it up. The Negro delivery boy brought her the package; the druggist didn't come back. When she opened the package at home there was written on the box, under the skull and bones: "For rats."

IV

So the next day we all said, "She will kill herself"; and we said it would be the best thing. When she had first begun to be seen with Homer Barron, we had said, "She will marry him." Then we said, "She will persuade him yet," because Homer himself had remarked—he liked men, and it was known that he drank with the younger men in the Elks' Club—that he was not a marrying man. Later we said, "Poor Emily" behind the jalousies as they passed on Sunday afternoon in the glittering buggy, Miss Emily with her head high and Homer Barron with his hat cocked and a cigar in his teeth, reins and whip in a yellow glove.

Then some of the ladies began to say that it was a disgrace to the town and a bad example to the young people. The men did not want to interfere, but at last the ladies forced the Baptist minister—Miss Emily's people were Episcopal—to call upon her. He would never divulge what happened during that interview, but he refused to go back again. The next Sunday they again drove about the streets, and the following day the minister's wife wrote to Miss Emily's relations in Alabama.

So she had blood-kin under her roof again and we sat back to watch developments. At first nothing happened. Then we were sure that they were to be married. We learned that Miss Emily had been to the jeweler's and ordered a man's toilet set in silver, with the letters H. B. on each piece. Two days later we learned that she had bought a complete outfit of men's clothing, including a nightshirt, and we said, "They are married." We were really glad. We were glad because the two female cousins were even more Grierson than Miss Emily had ever been.

So we were not surprised when Homer Barron—the streets had been finished some time since—was gone. We were a little disappointed that there was not a public blowing-off, but we believed that he had gone on to prepare for Miss Emily's coming, or to give her a chance to get rid of the cousins. (By that time it was a cabal, and we were all Miss Emily's allies to help circumvent the cousins.) Sure enough, after another week they departed. And, as we had expected all along, within three days Homer Barron was back in town. A neighbor saw the Negro man admit him at the kitchen door at dusk one evening.

And that was the last we saw of Homer Barron. And of Miss Emily for some time. The Negro man went in and out with the market basket, but the front door remained closed. Now and then we would see her at a window for a moment, as the men did that night when they sprinkled the lime, but for almost six months she did not appear on the streets. Then we knew that this was to be expected too; as if that quality of her father which had thwarted her woman's life so many times had been too virulent and too furious to die.

When we next saw Miss Emily, she had grown fat and her hair was turning gray. During the next few years it grew grayer and grayer until it attained an even pepper-and-salt iron-gray, when it ceased turning. Up to the day of her death at seventy-four it was still that vigorous iron-gray, like the hair of an active man.

From that time on her front door remained closed, save for a period of six or seven years, when she was about forty, during which she gave lessons in china-painting. She fitted up a studio in one of the downstairs rooms, where the daughters and grand-daughters of Colonel Sartoris' contemporaries were sent to her with the same regularity and in the same spirit that they were sent to church on Sundays with a twenty-five-cent piece for the collection plate. Meanwhile her taxes had been remitted.

Then the newer generation became the backbone and the spirit of the town, and the painting pupils grew up and fell away and did not send their children to her with boxes of color and tedious brushes and pictures cut from the ladies' magazines. The front door closed upon the last one and remained closed for good. When the town got free postal delivery Miss Emily alone refused to let them fasten the metal numbers above her door and attach a mailbox to it. She would not listen to them.

Daily, monthly, yearly we watched the Negro grow grayer and more stooped, going in and out with the market basket. Each December we sent her a tax notice, which would be returned by the post office a week later, unclaimed. Now and then we would see her in one of the downstairs windows—she had evidently shut up the top floor of the house—like the carven torso of an idol in a niche, looking or not looking at us, we could never tell which. Thus she passed from generation to generation—dear, inescapable, impervious, tranquil, and perverse.

And so she died. Fell ill in the house filled with dust and shadows, with only a dod-dering Negro man to wait on her. We did not even know she was sick; we had long since given up trying to get any information from the Negro. He talked to no one, probably not even to her, for his voice had grown harsh and rusty, as if from disuse.

She died in one of the downstairs rooms, in a heavy walnut bed with a curtain, her gray head propped on a pillow yellow and moldy with age and lack of sunlight.

V

The negro met the first of the ladies at the front door and let them in, with their hushed, sibilant voices and their quick, curious glances, and then he disappeared. He walked right through the house and out the back and was not seen again.

The two female cousins came at once. They held the funeral on the second day, with the town coming to look at Miss Emily beneath a mass of bought flowers, with the crayon face of her father musing profoundly above the bier and the ladies sibilant and macabre; and the very old men—some in their brushed Confederate uniforms—on the porch and the lawn, talking of Miss Emily as if she had been a contemporary of theirs, believing that they had danced with her and courted her perhaps, confusing time with its mathematical progression, as the old do, to whom all the past is not a diminishing road, but, instead, a huge meadow which no winter ever quite touches, divided from them now by the narrow bottleneck of the most recent decade of years.

Already we knew that there was one room in that region above stairs which no one had seen in forty years, and which would have to be forced. They waited until Miss Emily was decently in the ground before they opened it.

The violence of breaking down the door seemed to fill this room with pervading dust. A thin, acrid pall as of the tomb seemed to lie everywhere upon this room decked and furnished as for a bridal: upon the valance curtains of faded rose color, upon the rose-shaded lights, upon the dressing table, upon the delicate array of crystal and the man's toilet things backed with tarnished silver, silver so tarnished that the monogram was obscured. Among them lay a collar and tie, as if they had just been removed, which, lifted, left upon the surface a pale crescent in the dust. Upon a chair hung the suit, carefully folded; beneath it the two mute shoes and the discarded socks.

The man himself lay in the bed.

For a long while we just stood there, looking down at the profound and fleshless grin. The body had apparently once lain in the attitude of an embrace, but now the long sleep that outlasts love, that conquers even the grimace of love, had cuckolded him. What was left of him, rotted beneath what was left of the nightshirt, had become inextricable from the bed in which he lay; and upon him and upon the pillow beside him lay that even coating of the patient and biding dust.

Then we noticed that in the second pillow was the indentation of a head. One of us lifted something from it, and leaning forward, that faint and invisible dust dry and acrid in the nostrils, we saw a long strand of iron-gray hair.

Assignment Memo

Even though Emily Grierson is dead, we still want to prove that she committed the murder of Homer Barron. His family has hired us to discover the truth and to bring shame to the Grierson family. Please prepare an essay that organizes and presents evidence tending to show that she is the killer. You need to focus on evidence that shows why we should believe that she is the killer and how she carried out the crime. Avoid discussing her motives for now. All of the evidence that can be obtained is circumstantial. In addition to presenting the evidence in your essay, you should assess how strong or weak you believe it to be. The thesis of your essay will voice your overall assessment of how strong the case against her is.

Critiquing a student's use of quotations

Consider the following beginning of an answer and critique its weaknesses. Hint: Look for problems with the thesis, transitions, the way quotes are introduced, the way quotes are punctuated, quotes that are not necessary, quotes that are lacking, and evidence that is not specific enough.

Evidence against Emily Grierson

The group of townspeople who entered the house of recently deceased Emily Grierson received a gruesome surprise. The body of Homer Barron, long presumed to have left the town, was found dead in Grierson's bed. Worse, he had been dead for many years. Who killed him?

There is evidence about the body itself and its identity. "There was one room in that region above stairs which no one had seen in forty years." This means that since the body was found in that room, only Emily could have been involved. The body was in the kind of condition that means it must have been there a long time and could not have just died recently of natural causes. There is no evidence to show that the body is that of Homer Barron. The stuff found in the room could belong to anyone, and as for the only items that could have identified him: "so tarnished that the monogram was obscured."

Assignment Memo

The Barron family has realized that if Grierson can be shown to have premeditated the homicide, it will be considered a first-degree murder. A key component in proving premeditation involves establishing the motive behind the killing. Our team has done a preliminary analysis of the facts and determined three major categories of motive in this killing. 1) As a prominent citizen of a small and highly gossipy small town, Grierson was under constant public surveillance and social pressure, which caused her to snap when exposed to disgrace; 2) Grierson was dominated by her father, who stunted her emotional growth and left her unable to cope without a male in charge of her life; and 3) Grierson was so stuck in the world of the past that she could not accept any form of change and would do anything to preserve things the way they were.

Please write an essay analyzing Grierson's possible motives by exploring each of those three ideas, one per paragraph. For each, look for evidence that shows it is true and present the evidence in detail. Remember that the essay must begin with a paragraph that states a thesis and end with one that states a conclusion.

Assignment Memo

Grierson's family has hired us to clear her name. They have this idea that Grierson is a kind of feminist role model striking back at the men in her life by using their stereotypical ideas about women against them. They say that on multiple occasions, Grierson used the fact that she was a woman to make her crime possible.

Their ideas intrigue me. Please write an essay trying to prove their claim with detailed evidence.

UNITY

What is unity?

A paragraph achieves **unity** when it is devoted to a single purpose, and any sentences unrelated to that purpose are eliminated. As you revise your own writing, you must attack each sentence and ask it the question, "What are you doing in this paragraph?" If no direct connection can be made to that paragraph's topic sentence, the sentence has to go.

Critiquing a student's presentation of evidence for lack of unity

For each sentence, give an explanation as to why it does or does not belong in the paragraph by deciding whether it is helping to support the topic sentence.

Emily Grierson's strange interactions with other people provide evidence that she was insane throughout most of her life. Her manner of acting with the councilmen who tried to collect her taxes was very strange. "I have no taxes in Jefferson." Some may say she was just being aggressive, but it seemed to go beyond that. Emily's family had always been very proud. Her behavior after her father's death was also not normal. The death of a loved one can be very painful, and reactions can be surprising. However, few people carry it to such extremes. For three days, she had "the ministers calling on her." Her conduct with her father's body is similar to what happens with Homer Barron's body, in fact. Emily's house was allowed to fall into terrible decay. She let her body go. Even simple interactions with people like the chemist were abnormal: "I want arsenic."

As a follow-up, identify where you see any of the following problems in the Student Writing above: 1) need for more specific evidence, 2) problems introducing and integrating quotations.

Chapter

7 Gathering Research
Immigration

RESEARCH PAPER VS. INFORMATION DUMP

In grade school, many students get the idea that a research paper consists of information obtained from outside sources and stitched together to form a "report." They are shocked when their college instructors reject this.

It's important to realize that a college-level research paper is supposed to be **your** paper, representing your ideas and arguments. The research must play a supporting role, being brought in to help prove the truth of what you are saying. It must not be allowed to **be** what you are saying.

It is your job to keep the research from taking over the paper. You do this in several ways: limiting the amount of space devoted to researched material, integrating the research in a way that makes it less important than your own writing, and basing your essay on strong ideas of your own. An essay that has failed to keep control over its research sources risks turning into a glob of facts with the student's ideas totally absent—that is, an information dump.

THE CASE FOR PRINT SOURCES

When the Internet was new, it was greeted with great suspicion by academia. Students were urged to avoid it as a source of information. Even today, most professors express a strong preference for print sources and may ban web sources outright. There are some valid reasons for this policy.

- Print sources are typically subjected to an editing process by experts. Web sources can be self-published by people who don't know what they are talking about, and they may not be reviewed for quality or accuracy.
- A print writer usually needs a minimal amount of credibility to even get printed. Anyone can publish on the web.

- Print resources will stay around for a very long time should some-one want to consult them. Someone following up on your web source may find it gone the next day (or minute).

This doesn't mean you should be irrationally afraid of Internet sources as long as your instructor allows them. However, ensure the quality of your information by addressing those concerns:

- Choose materials that have been reviewed by some kind of board or community. Look for signs of quality control.
- Know who is writing the material, what credentials they have, and what agenda they might be pursuing. Investigate the author and use unsigned material only if you can learn something about the agency that produced it.
- Look for materials with an air of permanence. The best way to do this is to choose materials that are already in print and that you have accessed on the Internet only for convenience.

LOCATING PRINT SOURCES

One of the principal reasons students shun print sources is the belief that they are difficult to locate. Each library has its own online catalog, though they are all increasingly similar to the major search engines familiar to Internet users. Your best guide here is the library staff itself, which may offer orientation sessions and is always available to answer your questions.

Be aware that most libraries have a section of "reference materials" that cannot be removed from the library. These can usually be identified because the Call Number, the series of letters and digits used to locate the material, will begin with the letters "REF." Also be aware that older materials may exist only in microfilm and microfiche, film strips and plastic cards with miniaturized text that must be fed through a reading machine to be viewed. This may seem hopelessly antiquated, but for very specialized research tasks it may be the only option.

LOCATING INTERNET SOURCES

Though using a search engine such as Google doesn't require any specialized training, a few little-known tips can help you sort through the millions of results you will often get. Not everyone knows that . . .

Search terms can be excluded

You can force Google to exclude a certain search term by putting a minus sign (-) in front of it. If I am searching for contract disputes, and there is a famous golf player named Contract Jones who recently had a scandalous dispute, pages on that subject will crowd out what I really want. I can solve the problem by searching for *contract disputes -golf.*

Search terms can be specified in groups

If you only are interested in certain terms when they are next to other certain terms, you can use quotation marks around the whole group of terms. If I really do want to know about the golfer Contract Jones, but don't want information about contracts, then I'll search for *"Contract Jones."* In contrast, considering the previous tip, a search for golfers *-"Contract Jones"* would tell me about all golfers except Contract Jones.

Search terms can be limited to a specific site

If you want to search for a term, but only within a specific website, use the *site:* operator. If I wanted to see laws about bigamy, but only from the site that carries the official U.S. laws, I would search for *site:www.leginfo.ca.gov bigamy.* This would keep me from having to wade through other sites that perhaps have commentary on the laws but not the laws themselves.

Other tips for Internet searches

You can get these same options through a user-friendly form by clicking *Advanced Search* when you are on Google's home page. This form lets you set still more options, such as specifying a range of dates to include or exclude.

Here's another tip to cut millions of results down to a relevant few. Try to imagine a phrase that would *have to be* included on a website for you to find that site useful. For example, if you wanted to find out if it was possible to have a legally binding wedding over the Internet, searching for *legal wedding Internet* or *marriage web* could bring up all kinds of things. Instead, ask yourself what kind of phrase you'd expect a relevant page to contain. For example, you might expect such a page to contain the words, *"get married online."*

One last under-utilized tip: Once you have found a web page you want to visit, instead of wasting time scrolling all over the page to find the part that interests you, use your browser's search function. For most browsers, it is activated with Ctrl-F. Then you can enter the key word or phrase and jump directly to it.

Advanced Internet search techniques applied to the laws on prostitution

To test your understanding, consider what search terms you would enter in a search engine such as Google under the following circumstances:

Task	Search Terms
You want to find groups that help provide legal defense for arrested prostitutes, but all you find are groups that advocate to legalize prostitution.	
You want to learn about the laws of prostitution for California, but all your searches keep bringing up ads for prostitution.	
You want to learn which countries treat prostitution as a minor infraction, but you keep getting laws about prostitution committed with a minor.	
You want to find examples of laws around the world that make it a prostitution offense to offer to provide sexual services even if the agreement is not carried out.	

Managing information from web sources

Once you find good information, it's highly advisable to copy and paste it into a word processing document for future reference. This is better than just bookmarking the page because you won't have to scour through the page next time. But don't forget: whenever you copy and paste information from the web, also note the important information about the source that you'll need later to cite your sources: the author, publisher, title, date of creation, date of access, and URL (see page 117 for more about citation). This will also save you later hassle.

Many great online utilities exist to help you manage web findings without having to fuss with a word processing document that might not always be available to you. Evernote is a popular one.

All of these options are preferable to printing out enormous amounts of information on paper, which is wasteful of resources and harmful to the environment.

EVALUATING INTERNET SOURCES

Before deciding to rely on a given site for information, subject it to an investigation based on questions of who, what, why, how, and when?

Who?

Is there an identifiable person or organization claiming credit for the information? Can you find information about that person's or organization's credentials?

Even the URL (the web address) can give some clues as to who is behind the site: .gov sites are from a governmental agency; .com sites are commercial in nature; .org sites are non-profit; and .edu sites are from educational entities. But be careful with assumptions you draw from this. A non-profit site can be even more biased than a commercial one. An .edu site has work from professors, but also from first-year students.

Above all, remember that a prime objective for misleading sites is to disguise their origin. Press hard to verify who is really behind the site by using a search engine to go OUTSIDE the site and investigate the names of groups and people involved.

What?

Looking at the content itself, does the wording have a professional tone? Is it free of errors? Does the page look as if it were designed by professionals with high standards?

Why?

Do you see signs of bias through one-sided, emotional language? Bias can also be detected by looking at what sites link to or from this site or by investigating the groups that fund, host, sponsor, or create the material.

When?

How recent is this information? Keep in mind that having recent information is more important for some subjects (such as current laws or statistics) than for others (such as simple, general information like the dates of historical events). Not all pages will tell you directly when they were last updated, but you can find clues in such things as numerous broken links or other signs that the page has not been attended to in a long time.

A FEW WORDS ABOUT WIKIPEDIA

Wikipedia is a free, collaborative Internet encyclopedia, composed of millions of articles that are submitted and edited by volunteers from all over the world. Unlike a traditional encyclopedia, Wikipedia has no mechanism for monitoring the credentials of its contributors and no central authority that gives final review or approval to the articles. It has been praised as a model of cooperative research by and for the people, but in academic circles it has come under intense criticism. The ease with which false information can work its way into the articles and the anonymous nature of its contributors have caused many professors to forbid its use in college writing.

This, of course, has not stopped students from using it. Rather than pretend that the site doesn't exist, it seems wise to set out a few guidelines for its effective use.

- Realize that Wikipedia is an excellent source for more recent updates and more information rooted in popular culture than a traditional encyclopedia is likely to offer.
- Use Wikipedia to get a preliminary idea of important issues, but plan to use other sources to explore those issues.
- Explore the sources that Wikipedia refers to within its articles rather than trusting the articles themselves.
- Verify information taken from Wikipedia by consulting other, more stable and respected sources.
- Feel reasonably confident in trusting Wikipedia for answers to general questions.

It should also be mentioned that many of Wikipedia's foes do not have a clear understanding of how the site works. With the incredible volume of users on most pages, inaccuracies are often spotted within minutes of being posted. Articles that trigger controversy are linked to discussion pages where users debate and present evidence to arrive at the truth. Often, reading these discussions can be extremely informative. Thus, Wikipedia does, in fact, have a review process that can operate far more quickly than a traditional encyclopedia, and it offers an opportunity to peek inside the process of construction that print sources could never provide.

A RESEARCH TASK: ASYLUM

Gathering and evaluating sources for an asylum case

Assignment Memo

As you know, the United States may sometimes grant political asylum to non-citizens who are present and fear returning to their own country. To receive such a status, a petitioner has to build a strong argument that they face persecution and danger back home, and that the United States offers them their only chance at safety.

A strong case requires a convincing narrative of the petitioner's experience, but also research that portrays the home nation as a dangerous place. This danger has to be specific to the petitioner, but we have all kinds of petitioners asking for our help. Therefore, I would like you to compile research that will help show all the significant dangers of a certain country. You can choose which country to focus on.

Someone else will do the writing on this assignment. Your job is just to compile a list of websites that are reliable sources of information. Please list five websites and your full evaluation of their quality. So that we can get an idea of your standards, please include two "bad" sites among these five for comparison purposes.

Review: critiquing a student's narrative for an asylum case

Earlier, we looked at some guidelines for constructing an effective narrative (page 65). With those guidelines in mind, consider the following assignment.

Assignment Memo

Our client, Ezekiel, is seeking asylum in our country due to persecution in his home nation. He was asked to provide a narrative, but what he came up with is confusing, vague, and unhelpful to his case. Please identify the weaknesses in his narrative and provide recommendations for how to improve it. We are looking for moments where the facts are confusing or where he has failed to give a clear account of the events. You may also find problems with fragments, run-ons, and parallel structure that add to the confusion. This is extremely important, as the success of his case will hinge largely on the effectiveness of this narrative.

Ezekiel's Asylum Narrative

I was an elected government official for four years, founded a prestigious educational academy, and a major hospital in 1976. I studied from 1965 to 1972 at the City University, graduating as a teacher, studying for a degree that was received in mathematics. I entered politics in 1985 with the Union Leader and the General Secretary, Aaron Lopez. Winning the elections in 1987.

I participated in various reform movements, chosen by the Political Action Committee, I was very successful. Committee members admired his energy, encouraged him to get more experience, and skills. Eventually, I began to speak out against General Fuentes and the President of the country. Accused of many crimes.

One day I was pursued by many people in a vehicle when I came out of a talk that I had been giving because I had been invited the day before. This was in response to a similar talk I had given a month earlier when there had also been an attempt against my life. I headed for home to get my wallet. We headed toward the river. These fellows stopped me and tied me. They told my brother to leave, my wife cried for help, yelling that they would kill her, they silenced her. We complained, but nobody did anything until two months later. They did not take us seriously. The only reason we got away was because of the distraction. This all happened on the hottest day of the year, and I was sweating so hard that I could not see clearly. They forced me to stare straight into the sun.

Some people were yelling. Outside my house. I went to investigate and found a demonstration in progress. Since this was late at night, the demonstrators were breaking the law. There is a law against assembling late at night. Meeting at the foot of the pier. I called my colleague to join me, and when he answered his phone I told him about the demonstration. We went down the main street carefully and listed everyone we could recognize, The mayor's sister, the mayor's brother-in-law, laughing loudly, there were dozens of others. Some were worse than others. That's when the army came in and repressed them. I went up to the mayor's brother and told him to explain what was going on as officers took me away and said to stop resisting them.

After I got out, I received many threatening phone calls, so I never answered the phone. Then I got a call threatening my family. At the same time, my political enemies gained power in the legislature taking all but a few seats. 23 seats.

I got a letter telling me to stop interfering, threatening my wife, and leave the country. They said I should know that my place was to be quiet and not thinking that I was the president. They said they would kill me, controlling and watching me.

As I was driving to work down the National Highway, six men grabbed me out of my car and covered our faces. They said we had wasted their time, irritated their boss, and more things than any of their enemies had ever done. Then a cell phone rang. It was the one in charge. After the phone call, we were seized again. When I woke up I was bleeding. I tried to get out, but it was impossible. Eventually, we were rescued.

I will never stop fighting for what I believe. This is how I feel, as long as they are in power, there is a threat where I am involved.

THE STRUCTURE OF EXEMPLIFICATION

Much of college writing consists at least in part of providing examples to illustrate the truth of your claims or the weight of your arguments. Here are a few tips that will improve your writing when you are trying to prove something through examples. Keep them in mind for assignments like the one above.

- Provide an "adequate" number of examples. One is almost never enough unless it is amazingly dramatic and informative. After three, the reader may start to get bored. You have to judge how many examples will be enough to convince or inform the reader.
- Provide a variety of examples. Though multiple examples of the same kind become repetitive, examples of different kinds are always helpful. Combine quotes from prominent authorities with statistics, personal experiences, large-scale trends, and individual cases. Combine famous with obscure and scientific proof with popular opinions. Don't rely exclusively on any one type.
- Make sure each of your examples is clearly related to the point you are making. Only share the information that is relevant.

Gathering, evaluating, and using sources for an asylum case

Presenting a convincing narrative is only one important element of a good asylum case. It's also necessary to show that conditions in the home country are particularly dangerous for someone of the petitioner's status. This status might refer to political opinion, race, religion, national origin, gender, or sexual orientation, among other things.

Assignment Memo

Our client is seeking asylum under the claim that he is homosexual [or choose a different status that you or your instructor specify] and that conditions in his home country of [choose a country or use the country that your instructor indicates] are too dangerous for people of his sexual orientation. However, this is highly debatable, and only about 50% of petitions based on sexual orientation in that country are being granted. Please do some research and compile an essay that will convince its readers that the country of our client's origin is extremely dangerous for homosexual persons. Be sure to use only the most reliable sources.

THE STRUCTURE OF ARGUMENTATION

Avoiding logical fallacies

Arguments are won through a convincing presentation of examples (see previous section), a controlled appeal to the reader's emotions (without becoming hysterical, overly sentimental, or preachy), and a tight control over logic. Following is a list of common *logical fallacies;* that is, errors in logic that weaken or destroy a writer's credibility.

Appeal to tradition: This occurs when a writer argues that because we have always done something, we should continue to do it. Though this is not an entirely unpersuasive tactic, acting as though it is the final answer to a controversy is a fallacy. Example: "We should ban same-sex marriage because since time immemorial, marriage has been between a man and a woman."

Ad hominem: This occurs when a writer directs his criticism against the personal attributes of someone instead of against the views or ideas of that person. This could be somewhat valid if the criticism calls into doubt the person's honesty or impartiality, but it is almost always a distraction from the main issue at hand and should be avoided. Examples: "The government attorney arguing against this asylum case once received asylum himself." Or "The government attorney arguing against this asylum case cheats on his taxes."

Argument based on ignorance: This occurs when a writer states that since there is no proof that he is wrong, he must be right. This may or may not be a fallacy, depending on the situation. If a woman is accused of being an unfit mother without any proof, she is entitled to say that, until proof is produced, a court cannot rule against her. In that situation, it is the accuser who would be in danger of committing the fallacy. Example: "This woman has no proof that she is a good mother, so she must be unfit."

Appeal to pity: This occurs when a writer relies exclusively on emotional appeal with no grounding in fact. This is not to say that emotion has no place in an argument, but that it must always be supported with facts and logic. Example: "If we declare him guilty, his parents will be devastated."

Bandwagon fallacy: This occurs when a writer bases his claim on the mere fact that many or even a majority of people agree with it. In a world where illiteracy and ignorance are rampant, such a strategy is almost always problematic. Example: "This law must be just because the people have spoken through their votes."

False authority: This occurs when a writer looks to an outside authority to solidify a claim, but that authority has no expertise or relevance to the claim under discussion. Of course, use of authority is very important in argument as long as those authorities are well chosen. Example: "The seriousness of the situation in Pandoria has been verified by several prominent talk show hosts as well as by my mom."

Circular argument: This occurs when a writer takes something he is trying to prove, assumes it is true, and then uses it as part of his proof. This is never good. Examples: "Asylum should never be granted because it allows people to stay here when they have no right to do so." "Citizens of that country should be allowed to seek asylum because of the high danger there. The danger can be proven by the high number of people from there who seek asylum." "The petitioner is lying when he says he is not a criminal. We know that he is lying because a police officer has said so. In judging between the two versions, we have to keep in mind that the petitioner is a criminal."

Either/or argument: This occurs when a writer acts as if the answer must be one of two options, ignoring that there may be other possibilities. This is dishonest. Example: "Either we must believe this police officer, or we must disbelieve all police officers."

***Post hoc ergo propter hoc* argument:** This occurs when a writer argues that because event B happened after event A, this proves that B was caused by A. Sometimes it does turn out that two events are causally linked, but this has to be proven rather than just taken for granted, probably through multiple repetitions of related phenomena. Example: "Ever since the child went to live with his father, his math scores have improved. This proves his father is having some effect on his math abilities."

Generalization: This occurs when a writer sets out a claim in highly general terms with no effort to supply details, specifics, examples, or proof. This is a clear sign of an unprepared or deceptive writer. Example: "Asylum cases always end in disaster, so we should not grant them."

Non sequitir: This occurs when a writer produces a conclusion that does not follow (or may be totally unrelated to) what had been written just previously. Example: "With all the casualties we have been experiencing in our conflicts overseas, now would be a bad time to increase our accep-tance of asylum cases."

Slippery slope: This occurs when a writer insists that taking a cause of action will have various negative effects without proving that they are likely to happen. Example: "If we give custody of this child to the grandmother, thousands of grandmothers will come to court seeking custody of their grandchildren."

Straw man: This occurs when a writer claims that the opposition has made arguments that were never actually made. The writer then makes a big show of demolishing those arguments impressively, yet this proves nothing since the arguments were the writer's invention, not the opposition's. Example: "The opposition is against immigration, but no other country in the world forbids all immigration."

Assignment Memo

One of your colleagues has been asked to compile an argument for why our client, Adolpho, should be granted asylum from his home nation of Pandoria. Adolpho belongs to a religious sect known as the Sopofiles and claims that this sect is persecuted in Pandoria. Unfortunately, our colleague did a horrible job preparing this argument and has been dismissed from the firm. Please look over what has been written and identify the logical fallacies at work so that we can eliminate them.

Argument for Adolpho's Asylum Case

The situation for members of the Sopofiles sect in Pandoria is extremely grave, demanding that we provide asylum for its members. The situation is so bad that even Jake Thomas, star of the major motion picture *Pandoria's Innocents* which chronicles the terrible situation, has called for this measure to be taken. Even if our moral principles do not urge us to help, we should think of the effects that the Pandorian crisis is having on our own country. Since the oppression of Sopofiles began three years ago, our unemployment rate has risen by 4% and violent crime nationwide has increased by 6%. Sopofiles are peaceful people and do not practice any of the violence that other Pandorians tend to practice. The only way to protect them from the oppression they face at home is to bring every single one of them to this country.

If we reject this asylum case, we will be sending a message that religious persecution is not a valid cause for asylum and will be rejecting thousands of people fleeing horrific abuse. We may even end up sending back full U.S. citizens who originally received their legal status here through asylum, and this could open the door to stripping natural-born citizens of their citizenship as well. We must either grant this asylum case or admit that we do not believe religious persecution exists. The government may feel that the Sopofiles do not deserve to enter our country because they worship a female deity, but we must not allow our own religious beliefs to dictate the fates of others.

Note that our previous president spoke against granting asylum in cases such as these, an occasion on which he also outrageously advocated the legalization of heroin and the outlawing of bicycles. None of this is surprising, since he was fat and a bitter, frustrated old man. Because of people like him, innocent little babies are being mercilessly denied their rights, the food plucked right out of their defenseless hands by greedy and cruel oppressors.

Nobody has ever proven that granting too many asylum cases has a bad effect on society, so clearly it can only help. In fact, people granted asylum are so grateful that they go out of their way to contribute to society. Nine out of ten people surveyed agree, including the president of the National Dental Association. Furthermore, since time immemorial we have always provided asylum in cases of religious persecution. Above all, the most compelling reason to grant this asylum case is because it is the right thing to do.

Anticipating the opposition

No argument is complete unless it devotes time to examining the arguments of the opposing side. It may seem strange to give "air time" to your opposition by presenting their arguments, but failure to do so makes it seem as though you have no answer to their points and gives them an advantage. Just be strategic. Only bring up opposing arguments if you can immediately point out the flaws or logical fallacies in them. But don't put ridiculous arguments into the mouths of the opposition just to make them look foolish; doing so means committing the straw man fallacy yourself.

Assignment Memo

We have prepared a denial of an appeal from a Ms. Gomis who is seeking asylum. It occurs to me that some of our arguments are not as strong as they could be, and I would like to be prepared against counterarguments we may face. Please review the facts of the case; then read the denial. Afterward, use the facts of the case to find any flaws in the argument presented in the denial and prepare arguments in favor of Ms. Gomis.

Facts of the Case

from *Gomis v. Holder*, 571 F.3d 353 (4th Cir. 2009).

Francoise Anate Gomis, a native and citizen of Senegal, petitions for review of an order of the Board of Immigration Appeals (BIA) that affirmed the decision of the immigration judge denying her applications for asylum ***. Gomis contends *** that the BIA's finding that it is not more likely than not that Gomis will be subjected to female genital mutilation if returned to Senegal is not supported by substantial evidence ***.

I

*** [I]n June 2005, Gomis filed an application for asylum in which she claimed that she fled Senegal because her family wanted her to undergo female genital mutilation (FGM or circumcision) and participate in an arranged marriage. ***.

At the hearing before the immigration judge, Gomis testified that she was born in 1978 in Dakar, Senegal, and lived with her family in the outskirts of Dakar. She is single and does not have any children. Gomis and her family are members of the Djola ethnic group, which still practices FGM, and her father, who is a businessman, has two wives, both of whom are circumcised.

Relating her circumstances, Gomis testified that in June 1999, her parents took her from school so that she could undergo FGM and become married to a man in his sixties. In exchange for this marriage commitment, her parents accepted gifts from the man. Because Gomis desired to finish school and retain her independence, she went to the police to report her parents' intentions, but the police told her to return home and try to resolve the problem. *** On her uncle's advice, Gomis obtained a passport and left home in November 2000, initially hiding at a friend's house in Senegal. *** Once in the United States, Gomis worked for an employee of the International Monetary Fund for three years.

While in the United States, Gomis learned that her parents had forced her 15-year-old sister to undergo FGM before marriage and that when Gomis' brother filed a complaint with the police, he was told to go home.

Gomis gave her opinion that 80 to 100% of the Djola women have undergone FGM and have been forced to marry older men. According to Gomis, when a woman's parents were ready to have her undergo FGM, they would come to her room with other family members when she was asleep and take her away. She noted that some families have FGM performed on their daughters when they are young, while other families wait until just before their daughters' marriage.

She acknowledged, however, that the Senegalese government is against the practice. Yet, families continue the practice of performing FGM because of tradition. Gomis stated that because her family wanted her to undergo FGM, there was nowhere in Senegal she could live without fear of being subjected to it. She stated that her family is widely dispersed throughout Senegal and that the country is small, where everyone knows each other.

***

In addition, Gomis presented other letters and documents confirming some of her testimony. She submitted her sister's medical file documenting her sister's visit to the doctor with medical complications after the circumcision; an attestation from her uncle stating that he helped Gomis leave Senegal to go to the United States; an attestation from the person who hired Gomis as a domestic servant, claiming that Gomis' uncle arranged for the employment; a letter sent to Gomis from her aunt in Senegal, who stated that her fiancé provided a dowry and that all the other women her age have been circumcised; a letter from her mother telling her that she cannot avoid customs, that her fiancé is losing patience with her, and that the entire village is laughing at her family; a letter from her father ordering her to return home so that she can be circumcised and marry her fiancé; and finally a letter from her uncle stating that he had seen her parents, and they had not changed their minds and continue to want Gomis to undergo the procedure.

The Department of State's report on FGM in Senegal, dated June 1, 2001, which was entered into the record, states that FGM is most common among Muslim groups in the eastern part of the country, but that most Senegalese women have not undergone the procedure and that it is becoming less common due to urbanization and education. The report refers to a study published in 1988, which found that only 20% of Senegalese women have undergone the procedure and which noted that other estimates place the figure between 5 and 20%. The report related that FGM is hardly practiced in populated urban areas. Regarding Gomis' ethnic group, the Djolas, the report states that rural elements of the Djola group practice FGM as a puberty initiation rite. For all of Senegal, 90% of the women who had undergone the procedure were between two and five years old at the time of the procedure, but for others it was part of a puberty initiation rite.

In 1998, Senegal's president called for the eradication of FGM, and since 1999, there have been programs and seminars to educate the public about it. Many rural villages have issued declarations against the practice. In January 1999, Senegal enacted a law criminalizing FGM with a sentence of one to five years' imprisonment. The report added that there had been no convictions under this law, and, because many of those circumcised were very young, they were not in a position to report violations.

Gomis also included in the record a State Department report on human rights conditions in Senegal, issued in March 2006, which stated that FGM was practiced in thousands of rural villages. It estimated that nearly 100% of the women in the northern Fouta region were FGM victims and that nearly 60–70% of the women in the south and southeast were. *** In addition, the report noted that 140 villages have renounced FGM but, nonetheless, many people were still practicing it.

***

Denial of Gomis Appeal

from: *Gomis v. Holder*, 571 F.3d 353 (4th Cir. 2009).

The record shows that the incidence of FGM in Senegal is low and that the practice hardly occurs in urban areas, such as Dakar. Further, most women have not been forced to undergo FGM, and the incidence of FGM is decreasing. Gomis, as an adult, is even less likely to be forced to undergo FGM because 90% of the women who undergo the procedure are between two and five years old at the time of the procedure. In addition, both practicing FGM and ordering FGM to be carried out on a third party are crimes, and prosecutors now bring criminal charges against perpetrators. Gomis was 29 years old when the BIA dismissed her appeal, and her family lives in Dakar. She is relatively well educated, especially in a country where the adult illiteracy rate approaches 40%, having had 12 years of schooling. The weight of the record evidence, including her age, her education, and the decreased incidence of FGM in Senegal, specifically in Dakar, supports the immigration judge and BIA's finding that it is not more likely than not that Gomis will face persecution.

***

Citing Sources
Intellectual Property

WHY MUST SOURCES BE CITED?

We live in suspicious times. Invariably, when sophisticated readers encounter information, they want to know where it came from so that they can decide how credible it seems to them. Furthermore, interested readers may well want to obtain the source material themselves to explore further into the subject. Just as importantly, creators of ideas and compilers of information deserve and require credit for the work they do. Failure to cite a source used in your essay constitutes a declaration that you came up with the material yourself, which is a fraudulent misrepresentation and a theft of intellectual property.

WHICH USES OF SOURCES MUST BE CITED?

On the one hand, the rule is simple. You must provide a ***citation*** that indicates the source of your material each and every time you draw on an external source. An external source is anything—a book, website, interview, article, television show—that was not created in your own mind on the present occasion.

On the other hand, the rule is complicated by the fact that use of sources to obtain general, widely available information does ***not*** require a citation. So what counts as general, widely available information? The test is not, "Would most people know this?" Rather, the correct question to ask yourself is, "Is this information that is likely to be obtained with exactly the same results from numerous different sources?" Let's try some examples.

Information	Needs to be Cited? Why/Why Not?
The border between the U.S. and Mexico is the longest land border in the Western Hemisphere.	Not necessary. This fact could be verified in any relevant source, and nobody "owns" the idea.
The border between the U.S. and Mexico is the most difficult to cross in the Western Hemisphere.	Necessary. Respected authorities could disagree on this evaluation.
The U.S. Department of State announces, "violence in Mexico has risen to an all-time high."	
The print media has been proven to exaggerate the scope and spread of recent violence in Mexico.	
Mexico consists of thirty-one states and a federal district.	
Seventy-two percent of Mexican citizens experienced some form of physical violence last year.	
The death penalty has not been applied in Mexico since 1961.	
Although 32,432 murders were reported last year in Mexico, reluctance to report crimes means that the figure is at least 10% higher.	
Fatalities related to drug trafficking in Mexico have reached alarming levels.	
Enormous numbers of people across the globe die every year in violent incidents.	
After visiting Mexico, one prominent journalist wrote a travel article calling it "very nice."	
Travel agencies cannot be seen as reliable sources when it comes to reporting the safety of a destination.	
One travel ad dismissed gang violence by saying that it was never directed at tourists.	

HOW ARE SOURCES PROPERLY CITED?

There are several different systems of citation widely used, and the choice depends on what field you are writing about. English papers are usually expected to use the system developed by the MLA (Modern Language Association). Papers in the social sciences are more likely to use the guidelines established by the APA (American Psychological Association), while the legal profession has several different citation systems to choose from, such as the ALWD Citation Manual.

We will focus on the MLA method, but once you have learned one system the rest are easy to adapt to. The most important thing to realize is that all citation methods are governed by strict rules designed to encourage maximum consistency.

What does an MLA citation look like?

MLA places a ***parenthetical citation*** in the text of the essay to indicate and document cited material. The underlying two principles are these: 1) put information about a source right next to the information cited, where it will be easy to see without interrupting the reading process; 2) put the bare minimum of information inside those parentheses to allow a reader to track down the source. If you remember those two principles, you will be able to master MLA citation by using common sense rather than by memorizing a catalog of rules.

Basic format for an MLA citation (omit the square brackets)

([Author's Last Name] [Page Number])

Sample: (Smith 32)

In the sample provided, the parenthetical citation is for a book or article written by someone whose last name is Smith, and the reference is to page 32. Place the parenthetical citation directly after the information being cited but before the sentence's period. If a quote is involved, never put the citation inside the quotation marks. Also, notice that no comma separates the name from the page number, and no abbreviation such as "p." or "pg." is used.

Placement of an MLA parenthetical citation

Seventy-two percent of Mexican citizens experienced "some form of physical violence last year" (Smith 32).

What if…?

For many sources, the basic format won't work. Internet sources are especially problematic. Check the following what-if scenarios when citing a source that presents problems.

What if my source…?	Solution	Example
has no author?	Leave out the author.	(32).
has two or three authors?	List them all.	(Smith, Jones, and Brown 32).
has more than three authors?	List the first, followed by *"et al."* This abbreviation simply means "and others."	(Smith *et al.* 32).
is not the only source by this author?	Include a comma and then the source's title after the author's name.	(Smith, *Danger** 32).
has no page number?	Use a paragraph or section number, prefacing the number with "par." or "sec."	(Smith par. 2).
has no numbering of any kind?	Leave out the number.	(Smith)
has no numbering AND no author?	List the title of the piece.	(*Danger**).

*When listing a title, you can use just one or more key words from the title, but don't shorten the words themselves. So the title *Danger in Foreign Lands* could be shortened to *Danger* but not to *Dang. For. Lnds.* Also, be sure to use the title of the piece, not the title of the publication (see page 121).

Redundant citations

When discussing how to introduce quotes (page 80), we saw that it's sometimes appropriate to mention the author's name as part of the sentence introducing the cited material. Any information mentioned in your own sentence can be omitted from the parenthetical citation within that sentence. However, it's bad style to mention page numbers in the sentence itself since the page number is probably not part of your main point.

Acceptable Variations in Parenthetical Citations

After visiting Mexico, one prominent journalist wrote a travel article calling it "very nice" (Smith 32).

After visiting Mexico, journalist Steve Smith wrote a travel article calling it "very nice" (32).

BUT NOT...

After visiting Mexico, journalist Steve Smith wrote a travel article and, on page 32, called it "very nice."

Another rule aimed to cut down redundancy says that if your whole paper is based on just one source, you can leave out the author and title and put just the page/paragraph number in each citation.

Also, if your essay draws from the same source for a while, instead of placing the same parenthetical citation after every sentence, you can wait until the last sentence that refers to that source and put the citation there. But remember:

- ■ If you are drawing information from different pages of the source, each change in page numbers will trigger a need for a new citation; and
- ■ If your use of a source is interrupted by even one reference to a second source, you will have to place enough parenthetical citations so that the reader can clearly see which material comes from which source.

1. All three of these quotes come from exactly the same source and page, so one citation can be used for all of them.

2. The Jones reference interrupts the Smith 32 references, which is why a citation for Smith 32 has to be used before and after it.

3. If the Jones reference hadn't been here, this citation could have been used for all four Smith 32 references.

4. This is still Smith, but now it's page 34, so a new citation is necessary.

5. This citation, which must be for a work without an author, applies to the quote in this sentence as well as the one in the previous sentence. The work apparently has no numbering.

Using One Citation to Apply to a Block of References

After visiting Mexico, one prominent journalist wrote a travel article calling it "very nice." He said he had "no problems." Everything was "just fine" (Smith 32).[1] Critics have called his optimism "foolish" (Jones 18).[2] However, Smith knew that he would have "harsh critics." He wrote, "I will prove them all wrong" (Smith 32).[3] In fact, he called his task of defying the critics one of his "guiding missions" (Smith 33).[4] A popular travel website calls Smith's calculations "entirely accurate." It praises him for his "honesty and bravery" (*Journalist in Mexico*).[5]

IMPORTANT: We have seen several situations where information can be left out; for example, when a source has no numbering system or when all your paper's citations are from the same author. But if you end up in a situation with ***nothing left*** to put in the parentheses, that's a problem. For example, what if your whole paper uses only one source, and that source has no numbering? It is not a good idea to put no citation at all because it starts to look like you are not giving due credit. If you have nothing else to put in a citation, at the very least put the author's name or, if that's not available, the title.

Long quotations

Any quotation that takes up more than four lines on a page is deemed a long quotation. They are best used sparingly. As seen in our discussion on when to quote (page 83), quotations can be disruptive. A reader faced with a long quote can be confused as to what part of the quote you want to draw attention to, and this can result in losing contact between the writer and reader.

A long quotation should be double-spaced, indented an inch from the left side, and begin and end on its own lines apart from the rest of your sentences. It should not be enclosed in quotation marks and, just to keep things interesting, the parenthetical citation at the end should go ***after*** the ending punctuation (period, question mark, or exclamation point). This is in contrast with other quotations, where the citation goes after the final quotation mark but before the ending punctuation. Introduce quotes like these just as any other, and do not let them float on their own.

Example of Long Quotation

My textbook has several things to say about MLA parenthetical citations:

> MLA places a ***parenthetical citation*** in the text of the essay to indicate and document cited material. The underlying two principles are these: 1) put information about a source right next to the information cited, where it will be easy to see without interrupting the reading process; 2) put the bare minimum of information inside those parentheses to allow a reader to track down the source. (Jung 32)

This seems simple enough, and I am looking forward to putting it into practice.

THE WORKS CITED LIST

Obviously, the parenthetical citation does not contain enough information for a reader to be able to track down the source and view it personally. For this reason, MLA requires that a ***Works Cited list*** be attached at the end of any essay that uses outside sources and that it include the complete information about each source. To build a Works Cited list, you need to know both the rules of how to format the overall list and the formulas for how to construct each individual entry.

Overall format of the Works Cited list

- Place the words "Works Cited" without quotation marks at the top of the page and center them.
- Double-space evenly throughout the list. Don't skip extra lines between entries.
- Use hanging indents, meaning that the first line of each entry goes flush left while any wrap-around lines are indented a half-inch.
- Alphabetize the entries according to the first word in each entry.
- Do NOT use bullet points or numbering.

Works Cited

Bell, Alice. *The Longest Day.* New York: Ace Publishing, 1922.

Gee, Graciela and Kevin Brace. "Measurements and Mistakes." *Psychology Online.* The Therapists Group, 2008. Web. 16 Mar. 2009. <http://www.psyon.com/~jj7212/gee.html>.

Lou, Lisa, Ann Brady and Florence Vishal-Godorsky. *A History of Rent Control in the Major Cities of the U.S.* New York: Beta Publishing, 1988.

Smith, Logan. "Causes of Unemployment Enrage Many but Surprise Few." *New York Times.* 22 Jun. 2010: B5+.

Titles of pieces vs. titles of publications

Before looking at how to format the individual entries of the Works Cited list, it's important to be clear on the rules for formatting titles. The general rule is that the titles of short works go in quotation marks, whereas the titles of long works are marked by italics (or underlining, but never both). This is not entirely helpful, as it leaves students guessing how short is short. Poems, songs, chapters, articles, and essays are short. Books, collections, albums, newspapers, and magazines are long.

A perhaps more useful general rule is that short works should be thought of as **Pieces** that are gathered together into containers or **Publications.** So a newspaper article is a Piece that belongs inside a newspaper, the Publication. An essay is a Piece that belongs inside a collection of essays, the Publication. Always put a Piece in quotation marks and the Publication in italics (or underline it, but do not do both).

Format of the individual entries in the Works Cited list

These rules are overwhelmingly numerous, as there is a huge variety of types of sources that an essay might use: books, interviews, films, pamphlets, court decisions, transcripts, etc. This book will not present the exhaustive rules because 1) they are widely available online, and 2) excellent online utilities now exist to take care of the formatting for you. We will examine only three of the most commonly encountered sources to give you an idea of how the system works. Complete guides to the MLA Works Cited rules can be found on numerous websites. Use a search engine to lead you to one.

For each of the formulas presented here, do not include square brackets. They are included only for clarity. Also, note that these are the simplest versions and that there are many variations depending on number of authors, presence of an editor, kind of periodical, etc. Again, use one of the many MLA guides available on the web for full details.

For a Book

Author's Last Name, Author's First Name. *Title.* Publisher's City:
     Publisher's Name, Publication Year.
Jung, Jeff. *Making the Best Case.* Dubuque: Kendall Hunt, 2011.

For an Article in a Periodical

Author's Last Name, Author's First Name. "Title of Piece." *Title of
     Publication.* Date of Article: Pages.
Jung, Jeff. "Using New Textbooks." *Education Monthly.* Dec. 2011: 32–56.

> ## For a Website
>
> Author Last Name, Author First Name. "Title of Individual Web Page."
>
> > *Title of Overall Website.* Sponsor of Site, Date of Last Update. Web.
> >
> > Date that Site was Accessed. <URL>.
>
> Jung, Jeff. "Using New Textbooks." *Education Monthly Online.*
>
> > Educational Press, 2011. Web. 13 Mar. 2011.
> >
> > <http://www.elcamino.edu/~jjung>.

Complications in identifying the elements of a website

Students quickly find that websites resist being categorized according to the pieces of data that MLA wants. Though some online sources are clearly articles that belong to a publication, others are harder or impossible to classify. In fact, not all pages even have a clearly identifiable title. It's not always obvious whether the page is a "Piece of a larger Publication" (see page 121) or if it stands alone. The reassuring solution: do your best.

The title of the Piece is often whatever is set in the largest font at the top. The title of the Publication can sometimes be found by following a link from the current page to the site's home page. Sometimes not. When all is said and done, the titles of online sources often are whatever you say they are. Just be sure to refer to any given source consistently the same way throughout all your references to it.

Automated citation utilities

Numerous software utilities exist that will prepare your Works Cited list and even help construct parenthetical citations. Word processors such as Microsoft Word offer such features, as do free websites that allow you to enter your information into a form and build the Works Cited list with the click of a button. Before you scream in frustration that there was no reason, then, to learn all the intricacies of how to build the list yourself, realize that these utilities are far from perfect. Before using them for long, you'll realize that you have to double-check everything they do, an impossible task unless you understand yourself what goes into the process and how to apply the rules.

Easybib, Bibme, Workscited4u, and Ottobib are highly popular. Some of these even allow you to bypass the chore of entering the various elements, instead entering a single ISBN (barcode number) for a book or the URL of a website. How does it manage to pluck the right information from a website and put each element in its proper category? Well, quite often it doesn't. The more automated the feature, the more need for you to double-check its work.

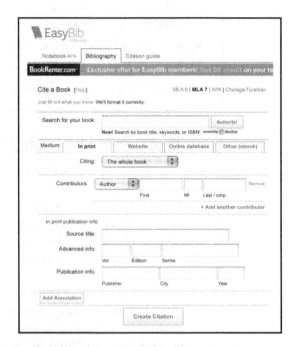

Screenshot of Easybib in Manual Mode

Extra practice with citations

1. Go back to the research that you compiled for the asylum case on page 105 ("Gathering and evaluating sources for an asylum case") and create a Works Cited list for the sources.

2. Go back to the research that you compiled for the asylum case on page 107 ("Gathering, evaluating, and using sources for an asylum case") and insert the appropriate parenthetical citations. Create a Works Cited list as well.

Chapter

9

Paraphrasing
Plagiarism · Intentional Torts

WHAT IS PARAPHRASING?

In our discussion about quoting, we emphasized that though use of specific evidence is always important, quoting is not always necessary. How do we introduce information from a source without quoting it? We ***paraphrase*** it, which is to say, we render it in our own words. The problem is that students vastly underestimate how much the wording must be revised in order to achieve a true paraphrase. Failure to paraphrase sufficiently opens a writer up to charges of plagiarism. Thus, we cannot fully master the technique of paraphrasing until we are clear on the concept of plagiarism.

WHAT IS PLAGIARISM?

Plagiarism is usually defined as the use of other people's words and/or ideas without giving credit in the attempt to pass them off as one's own invention. Note that this definition gives us a total of four ways to plagiarize.

- Copy someone's exact words without indicating that it is a quotation, even if you mention whose words they are.
- Paraphrase someone's words and fail to indicate whose they are no matter how extensively you changed the wording.
- Present someone else's ideas and fail to indicate whose they are no matter how extensively you changed the wording.
- Paraphrase someone's words but not extensively enough, even if you mention whose ideas they are.

Plagiarism is a very grave offense. The advent of the Internet has exposed higher education to a problem of epic proportions, as instructors find themselves deluged by a flood of stolen work cribbed from web pages or even bought from paper mills. Academia is fighting back hard by aggressively inspecting papers for signs of plagiarism using technology as well as common sense and pursuing harsh disciplinary measures that often include expulsion. As it is a form of fraud, it is not unheard of for a plagiarizer to face legal action as well. It is important to realize that academic institutions are not much interested in the excuse "I didn't realize I was plagiarizing because I thought I was just using research."

THE DIFFICULTY OF PARAPHRASING

Swapping out a few words for synonyms is not enough; in fact, swapping out a lot of words for synonyms is still not enough. Even rearranging the order of a few blocks of words is not enough. If your version "tracks" the original—that is, if it follows along the same general path and sequence of the original—it is plagiarizing.

A true paraphrase must completely take the original apart and put it back together again in an original way. This means ideas that are together in the original should be separated in the paraphrase, and ideas that were separate should be combined. Different grammatical patterns must be used, such as changing passive voice to active or taking what was originally a small phrase and expanding it into its own sentence.

Example of a True Paraphrase

Original: Plagiarism is a very grave offense. The advent of the Internet has exposed higher education to a problem of epic proportions, as instructors find themselves deluged by a flood of stolen work cribbed from web pages or even bought from paper mills.

Paraphrase: It seems that educators everywhere complain of enormous volumes of papers produced by dishonest means. Stealing work from the Internet has, of course, always been quite easy. Some students are even buying their papers outright from companies that specialize in their manufacture. It is safe to say that instructors are taking the problem of plagiarism very seriously.

Here are a few things to notice about this paraphrase. It keeps all the important information and does not add new facts to the original. However, it does add new phrases such as "it seems that," "of course," and "it is safe to say that." These help create a different rhythm without adding new meaning. The order of ideas is changed. The idea of stolen work is put in a different sentence from the bought papers. Passive voice has been changed to active—for example, "instructors find themselves deluged" becomes "educators everywhere complain." Most importantly, unusual words like "advent," "epic," "deluged," and "cribbed" are carefully avoided.

TIPS FOR HOW TO PARAPHRASE

A writer who wants to avoid plagiarism should follow these guidelines when paraphrasing:

- Study the original passage extensively, jotting down a few notes of the key concepts if you cannot keep it all in your head.
- Write your paraphrase *without looking at the original.*
- Compare your paraphrase with the original:
  - ☐ Make sure any unusual words in the original do not appear in your paraphrase
  - ☐ Try to add some unusual words and phrases in the paraphrase without changing the meaning
  - ☐ Make sure ideas are presented in a different, though still logical, sequence
  - ☐ For sentences that combine multiple ideas, try splitting them up or combining them in different ways

Most students resist the idea of writing the paraphrase without looking at the original. However, writing the paraphrase with the original still in view almost guarantees that you will end up with a result too similar to its source.

PRACTICE WITH PARAPHRASES AND PLAGIARISM

Assignment Memo

We need to hire an associate for our firm, and we need to make sure that we hire someone who knows the difference between appropriate paraphrasing and plagiarism. We asked five applicants to paraphrase a court opinion that ruled as to whether or not an insane person could be held liable for his torts (which are non-criminal harms inflicted on others, such as trespass, slander, or negligence). Please look at the five attempts and comment as to which ones successfully avoid plagiarism.

For the purposes of this task, don't worry about whether the paraphrase provides *all* the same information as the original. Just check to see whether they are plagiarism free.

Original Ruling written by Justice Qua

from *McGuire v. Almy*, 297 Mass. 323 (1937).

* * *

Turning to authorities elsewhere, we find that courts in this country almost invariably say in the broadest terms that an insane person is liable for his torts. As a rule no distinction is made between those torts which would ordinarily be classed as intentional and those which would ordinarily be classed as negligent, nor do the courts discuss the effect of different kinds of insanity or of varying degrees of capacity as bearing upon the ability of the defendant to understand the particular act in question or to make a reasoned decision with respect to it, although it is sometimes said that an insane person is not liable for torts requiring malice of which he is incapable. Defamation and malicious prosecution are the torts more commonly mentioned in this connection.

* * *

Five Attempts at Paraphrasing

1. Justice Qua noted that our country's courts almost invariably say that an insane person is liable for his torts. They might escape liability, though, for torts requiring malice of which they are incapable. Defamation and malicious prosecution would be examples.

2. Justice Qua considered the issue of insane people who commit torts. While noting that defamation and malicious prosecution require a malice that insane people cannot form, he said that most American legal authority sees no problem in holding them responsible for most other torts.

3. In his opinion, Justice Qua wrote that courts in this country almost invariably say in the broadest terms that an insane person is liable for his torts. He also said that no distinction is made between those torts which would ordinarily be classed as intentional and those which would ordinarily be classed as negligent.

4. Insane people are usually liable for their torts, whether intentional or negligent. It doesn't matter what kind of insanity is involved or how it interferes with their comprehension. The only exception might be for torts that require malice, like defamation and malicious prosecution, since insane people can't form malice.

5. Justice Qua noted that, turning to other authorities, our nation's courts almost always say very broadly that an insane person is liable for torts he commits. Generally, there is no difference between those torts that are normally called

intentional and those that are normally called negligent, nor do the courts discuss what effect different kinds of madness would have on the defendant's ability to comprehend a given act or to use reason to decide something about it. Sometimes, though, courts have ruled that an insane person is not liable for torts requiring malice that he cannot form. Defamation and malicious prosecution are examples of those kinds of torts.

Assignment Memo

Please paraphrase the three excerpts below.

from *Fisher v. Carrousel Motor Hotel*, 424 S.W.2d 627 (Tex. 1967)

[Context: This ruling decided that a person who grabs a plate from a defendant's hand can be held liable for battery, just the same as if he had laid hands directly on the defendant. The Texas Supreme Court is writing.]

***

Under the facts of this case, we have no difficulty in holding that the intentional grabbing of plaintiff's plate constituted a battery. The intentional snatching of an object from one's hand is as clearly an offensive invasion of his person as would be an actual contact with the body. "To constitute an assault and battery, it is not necessary to touch the plaintiff's body or even his clothing; knocking or snatching anything from plaintiff's hand or touching anything connected with his person, when done in an offensive manner, is sufficient." *Morgan v. Loyacomo, 190 Miss. 656, 1 So.2d 510 (1941).*

***

from *Harris v. Jones*, 380 A. 2d 611 (Md: Court of Appeals, 1977)

[Context: This ruling decided that an employee could not prevail in a suit for infliction of emotional distress against his employer who upset him by mocking his stuttering problem. The Maryland Court of Appeals is writing.]

***

While Harris' nervous condition may have been exacerbated somewhat by Jones' conduct, his family problems antedated his encounter with Jones and were not shown to be attributable to Jones' actions. Just how, or to what degree, Harris' speech impediment 573*573 worsened is not revealed by the evidence. Granting the cruel and insensitive nature of Jones' conduct toward Harris, and considering the position of authority which Jones held over Harris, we conclude that the humiliation suffered was not, as a matter of law, so intense as to constitute the "severe" emotional distress required to recover for the tort of intentional infliction of emotional distress.

* * *

from *Hackbart v. Cincinnati Bengals, Inc.*, 601 F.2d 516 (10th Cir. 1979)

[Context: This ruling considered the issue of whether a professional football player could sue another for injuries from a deliberate blow to the back of the head if the blow happened during a game but not as part of the game. The 10th Circuit Court of Appeals is writing about the ruling of the lower (trial) court, which had said that the plaintiff could not recover.]

* * *

Despite the fact that the defendant Charles Clark admitted that the blow which had been struck was not accidental, that it was intentionally administered, the trial court ruled as a matter of law that the game of professional football is basically a business which is violent in nature, and that the available sanctions are imposition of penalties and expulsion from the game. Notice was taken of the fact that many fouls are overlooked; that the game is played in an emotional and noisy environment; and that incidents such as that here complained of are not unusual.

* * *

Cause/Effect
Negligence · Insanity Defense

THE STRUCTURE OF CAUSE/EFFECT

One of the most common tasks required in writing is to demonstrate your understanding of either what factors caused a result or what results were caused by an event. Such an essay is usually easily organized by devoting one paragraph (or group of paragraphs) per cause/effect. The hard part is deciding what the causes and effects of any given event really are. Beware of the following traps that might weaken your essay.

Post hoc ergo propter hoc fallacy

Don't assume that just because one event occurred after another, the first event must have caused the second event. Even great philosophers and scientists have fallen into this trap, and the mass media commits it regularly.

Example: if five people in a city of 24,000 contract cancer, would it be reasonable to assume that the city's tap water caused their cancer?

Example: What should we make of the fact that when New York instituted a policy of cracking down on subway fare evasion, the rate of violent crime on the subway plummeted? It is a fallacy to just assume that the fare-evasion crackdown somehow caused the fall in crime without putting more thought into it. Of course, it could be true. But can you prove it? You would need to pose more questions:

- Has the same thing happened in other cities?
- Has it happened in New York more than once?
- Can you explain how the policy on fare evasion would have an effect on other crimes?

Answering yes to any of those questions helps remove your argument from the realm of *post hoc ergo propter hoc.*

Cum hoc ergo propter hoc fallacy

This similar error is committed when a writer assumes that because two events happen together, one must have caused the other. It may well be that what you have identified as the cause is really the effect. Or it may be pure coincidence or caused by some third factor.

Example: If neighborhoods where prostitutes walk the streets also have violent crime, is that because prostitutes attract the crime or because prostitutes feel less conspicuous in an area where more dangerous crimes are occurring? Or perhaps both the prostitutes and the dangerous criminals have been attracted to the neighborhood for another reason, such as its darkness, that has nothing to do with the other group.

Example: If neighborhoods with many police officers on the street have high crime rates, can we conclude that putting many officers on the street causes crime? It may be more reasonable to assume that the high number of officers is a result caused by the high crime. Then again, it may turn out that almost all the crime is directed against the police officers themselves (or committed by them!) in which case our first theory would have been right after all.

The problem of superseding causes

We first came across the concept of superseding cause when looking at the case of *Thief v. Victim* on page 58. The idea is that between a triggering cause and an eventual result, many other events may happen. If one or more of those events has a drastic enough effect on the eventual result, it makes more sense to identify the superseding cause as the "true cause."

Example: If New York cracks down on fare evasion, and this causes the city's most infamous mafia leader to get arrested while jumping a turnstile, which leads to the collapse of his mafia ring when his two sons kill each other over a leadership dispute, this will cause a reduction in crime as an eventual result. We could still say that the fare evasion crackdown was the cause of this crime reduction, but it now seems to be stretching a point. Nobody could anticipate that busting turnstile jumpers would lead to a blood feud in the mafia, and the true cause or ***proximate cause*** of the crime reduction is more likely to be considered the double murder of the leader's sons.

Tips for writing a cause/effect study

Ask yourself the following questions as you prepare your analysis:

- Have I really found all the causes and effects?
- Could my cause actually be an effect, or vice versa?
- Could some of my causes have causes of their own? Could my effects have more effects of their own?
- Do I have proof that this is not coincidence at work?
- Some instructions call for analysis of causes, others for effects, and others for both. Did I follow those instructions?
- Have I checked for superseding causes that may render the original causes irrelevant?
- Have I made it clear where I see a cause/effect as certain and where it is only a possibility?

NEGLIGENCE

Negligence occurs when a defendant does not act according to the standard of care that he owes to the people around him and when that lapse in care causes verifiable damage to someone. As we will see, the idea of "cause," as discussed, plays a big role in determining whether a person is liable for negligence. After learning a bit about the four elements that must be proven to win a negligence suit, we will examine a number of scenarios and determine whether any of the players in them can successfully sue for negligence.

To win a negligence suit, a plaintiff must convince the court that 1) the defendant owed him a ***"duty of care"***—that is, a certain level of responsibility to protect him from harm; 2) the defendant ***"breach***ed" that duty—that is, failed to exercise appropriate care; 3) the breach was the "***proximate cause***" of harm—that is, has no superseding causes that he can blame; and 4) ***damages*** resulted. We will take these one at a time.

Duty of care

A person cannot be sued simply because something he did played a part in someone's harm. There must first be something wrong with what he did. In legal terms, we ask whether the defendant had a duty of care toward the plaintiff. Ordinarily, all people are assumed to have a duty to refrain from acting in a way that creates substantial and unreasonable risks to other people. However, ordinarily we do not have a duty to take action to help others who are strangers to us.

Example: A person has a duty not to throw burning items out of second-story window, but a person who sees a passerby drowning does not traditionally have a legal duty to help (although individual state laws may change this).

Though some duties are easy to agree upon, such as a duty to drive safely, to practice a profession according to approved standards, or to keep a dog from attacking others, there are many gray areas. Courts generally argue that a person has a duty to refrain from conduct that is likely to cause significant harm, especially if the conduct is not socially important, not useful to the defendant, and easy and unburdensome to avoid.

Example: A person driving to the hospital while bleeding from a gunshot wound is doing something so important and (arguably) impossible to avoid that a court may say he has a reduced or no duty to drive according to the rules of the road. However, a person driving with his eyes closed to test his instincts will be expected to abide by the usual duty to drive safely.

In spite of the general rule that there is no duty to assist others, there are a number of exceptions. Among other reasons, people are expected to render assistance when 1) they have a special relationship such as parent–child or hotel owner–guest, or 2) the defendant actually played a role in creating the danger in the first place.

Example: A woman who sees a child playing with a blowtorch has no duty to stop him. However, she would have a duty if she were his mother or his caretaker or if she were the one who had given him the blowtorch or allowed him to have it.

Breach

Once a duty of care is established, the plaintiff will need to show that the defendant failed to abide by that duty, breaching it.

Proximate cause

The plaintiff needs to show that the harmful result would not have happened if it had not been for the defendant's conduct, or at least that the conduct played a substantial role in producing the result. Additionally, the plaintiff will have to prove that no superseding causes got in the way to take the blame away from the defendant. The rule is that an intervening cause is considered to be superseding and invalidates the negligence claim if it was unforeseeable and unrelated to the defendant's actions.

Example: A woman trips over a wastepaper basket that a negligent janitor left in the hallway. This delays her from exiting the building, and she is crushed 30 seconds later when the building collapses from an earthquake. The earthquake was not foreseeable, and it was not triggered in any way by the negligent placement of the wastepaper basket. The earthquake is an intervening cause that supersedes the janitor's negligence. The woman will have no case against him because he even though he breached his duty, he was not the proximate cause of her being crushed.

Example: A woman rushes to exit a building in the midst of an earthquake but cannot open the emergency door that has been negligently allowed to remain in disrepair. She is crushed 30 seconds later when the building collapses. Even though this particular earthquake was not foreseeable, the whole point of having an emergency exit is for incidents such as these. In this sense, injuries stemming from an earthquake or fire are foreseeable consequences of a defective emergency exit, and the earthquake is not really a superseding cause. If the woman sues her building's management company, nothing should prevent their negligent maintenance from being seen as the proximate cause of her being crushed.

Damages

Finally, a plaintiff will have to prove that damages resulted from the defendant's conduct. With rare exceptions, these have to be damages of physical injury or property damage. Mental suffering or economic loss, such as lost business opportunities, are normally not sufficient unless they are in combination with physical injury or property loss.

WRITING ABOUT NEGLIGENCE

Assignment Memo

Presumably, you are familiar with the four elements that a plaintiff must prove to win a negligence suit. Please read the following account of a family trip to the zoo that ended in death. According to the story, Jimmy, the son of Tom and Lisa, was killed. Now Lisa wants to file a negligence claim against her husband, holding him responsible for their son's death.

Your first task will be to study the story and list every action of Tom's that somehow played a part in Jimmy's death. Then write an essay discussing which of his actions could be seen as an example of negligence. Remember that an action will have to meet all four criteria, so you need to discuss all four criteria for each action. The hardest part will be in determining whether each action is truly a proximate cause of Jimmy's death or whether intervening causes were significant enough to be superseding. Please review the discussion of negligence on the preceding pages as necessary.

The Negligent Father

Tom was one of those people who always had to do things his way. He liked to carry his rifle with him everywhere he went because his state allowed it, and he wanted people to be informed of their right to carry weapons openly. His wife, Lisa, had told him that she didn't want him to bring his rifle with him when they went to the zoo because, as she said, it was heavy, it took up too much room in the car, and he looked like an idiot carrying it around everywhere. He solemnly promised her that he would leave it at home, but as they and their 8-year-old son, Jimmy, were getting out of the car at the zoo and unloading the trunk, it turned out that he had brought it along after all.

The day at the zoo was pleasant enough, but about ten minutes before closing, Tom decided that he really wanted to see the deadly reptile exhibit all the way on the other side of the zoo. "We can still make it if we run," he urged them. Complaining, but realizing there was no talking him out of it, Lisa did her best to keep up and to hurry Jimmy along. "Your shoelace is untied," she yelled after her husband, but he waved impatiently at her and ignored her words.

Arriving in triumph at the deadly reptile exhibit at a full sprint, Tom stepped on his untied shoelace and stumbled forward. He probably would have regained his balance if it had not been for some cleaning equipment that had carelessly been brought out and then left unattended. It was at this time about 30 seconds before the zoo's official closing. Tom tripped over this equipment and fell to the ground. Since he had failed to correctly secure the safety mechanism of the rifle, it fired, shattering a nearby glass aquarium and badly scaring the other visitors who had been peering into it. Tom was quite surprised, since he had emptied the rifle's ammunition earlier that morning. He did not know that little Jimmy had decided to reload it during the two minutes that Tom had left the rifle unattended while running to answer the phone.

One of the visitors who had been frightened by the glass shattering was visibly angry. He was a rather dangerous-looking man, heavy, imposing, and hostile. He lost no time in making his way over to Tom and letting him know in less than delicate language what he thought of him. Tom was in no mood. Rising to his feet, he began to enter into a shouting match that became more volatile by the second. Lisa, now arriving on the scene with Jimmy, erupted in disgust: "This is so typical. You're on your own. I'm not even getting into this." So saying, she marched off enraged, leaving Jimmy behind to witness his father's argument, which was beginning to turn into a fight.

Nobody seemed to notice that the deadly python that made its home in the recently shattered aquarium had slithered its way to freedom during the fight. The other visitors had fled the scene, and while Tom and his new foe grappled on the ground, the python silently wrapped itself around Jimmy. By the time Tom could be troubled to look up from his efforts, it was much too late.

Starting the assignment

The assignment memo itself suggests that we start the assignment with listing, a form of prewriting that we discussed on page 41. Below, write a list of Tom's actions that could conceivably be seen as the cause of Jimmy's eventual injuries. Don't try to analyze at this early stage whether there will be a convincing link. Our purpose is just to list every possibility.

Listing of Tom's Possibly Negligent Actions

1. Brought rifle to zoo when told not to.

2. _____

3. _____

4. _____

5. _____

6. _____

The structure for this essay has already been decided for us by the assignment memo itself. We will want one paragraph for each of Tom's problematic actions, and in each paragraph we will want to consider each of the four elements of negligence. Then we will tack on an introduction explaining the question and a conclusion summarizing the answer and giving our best prediction as to what fate will befall this Case of The Negligent Father.

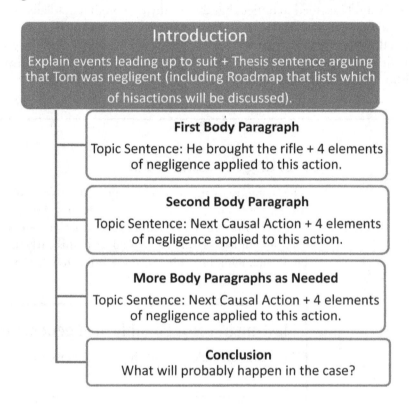

As we start the first body paragraph, let's see how far we can get with the first item on our list—the bringing of the rifle. We must first ask whether this involved a duty that Tom owed to his family, a duty that he failed to fulfill. Looking back to our definition of negligence that began on page 133, we see that all people have a duty to refrain from acting in a way that creates substantial and unreasonable risks to other people.

Was Tom's action so unreasonably dangerous as to violate that duty? That may be debatable since none of Lisa's reasons for asking him to leave the rifle at home were related to safety. Is carrying a rifle always unreasonably dangerous, no matter what? Does bringing it to the zoo make it more dangerous? As you can see, just the question of whether Tom had a duty to leave his rifle at home can be argued on both sides.

Let's assume for the moment that we believe bringing the rifle to the zoo was a breach of a duty of care. We now have to ask whether it was a proximate cause of Jimmy's death. Were there intervening causes between the bringing of the rifle and Jimmy's death? Clearly there were, such as Tom's tripping. Should we count that as superseding, or do you think it was foreseeable that under the circumstances a person might be expected to trip and, in so doing, cause his weapon to fire? There may be other intervening causes that you should consider as well.

What about the escape of a python? Is it foreseeable that bringing a rifle to the zoo may expose someone to the attack of a deadly reptile? In answering these questions, keep in mind that even if you decide one particular act did not make Tom negligent, you are still free to find him negligent through one or more of his other actions.

The final element, damages, is easy. Jimmy suffered physical injury and death. Since this part of the analysis is the same for every one of Tom's actions being analyzed (in each case, Jimmy was hurt the same way) you can simply say when discussing Tom's other actions that damages were discussed earlier and would be the same.

This should give you an idea of how to proceed. Now work through the other items on the list.

MORE PRACTICE WITH NEGLIGENCE

The following two cases will continue to test your ability to write about negligence claims. In both cases, a plaintiff has sought police protection unsuccessfully and suffered harm as a direct result of supposed police negligence. In the first case, *Riss v. New York,* a woman asked for protection from a threatening stalker, was denied, and suffered disfiguring injuries from the stalker; however, she lost her case. In the second case, *De Long v. County of Erie,* a woman whose house was being broken into called 911 but never received the requested help and was actually killed. Her husband sued the police for negligence and won.

Why was the plaintiff in *De Long* successful whereas the plaintiff in *Riss* was not? It could be because the police were only perceived to owe a reasonable duty, for some reason, in the *De Long* case; or perhaps they owed a duty in both cases but only did something wrong (breached) in *De Long.* Possibly there were superseding causes in the *Riss* case that prevented any improper police behavior from being considered the true cause of her injuries. To answer the question of why Mr. De Long prevailed while Ms. Riss lost, you will need to apply the ***definition*** of negligence and also carefully ***compare and contrast*** the two cases to see why they ended differently.

Assignment Memo

Read the following two cases and write an essay explaining why you believe Mr. De Long won while Ms. Riss lost. Structure your essay by comparing the two cases and using the definitions of negligence to analyze each outcome.

Riss v. City of New York

from *Riss v. City of New York*, 22 N.Y. 2d 579 (1968)

***

Justice Keating wrote this opinion to express his disagreement (dissent) with the court's ruling against Riss.

Linda Riss, an attractive young woman, was for more than six months terrorized by a rejected suitor well known to the courts of this State, one Burton Pugach. This miscreant, masquerading as a respectable attorney, repeatedly threatened to have Linda killed or maimed if she did not yield to him: "If I can't have you, no one else will have you, and when I get through with you, no one else will want you". In fear for her life, she went to those charged by law with the duty of preserving and safeguarding the lives of the citizens and residents of this State. Linda's repeated and almost pathetic pleas for aid were received with little more than indifference. Whatever help she was given was not commensurate with the identifiable danger. On June 14, 1959 Linda became engaged to another man. At a party held to celebrate the event, she received a phone call warning her that it was her "last chance". Completely distraught, she called the police, begging for help, but was refused. The next day Pugach carried out his dire threats in the very manner he had foretold by having a hired thug throw lye in Linda's face. Linda was blinded in one eye, lost a good portion of her vision in the other, and her face was permanently scarred. After the assault the authorities concluded that there was some basis for Linda's fears, and for the next three and one-half years, she was given around-the-clock protection.

No one questions the proposition that the first duty of government is to assure its citizens the opportunity to live in personal security. And no one who reads the record of Linda's ordeal can reach a conclusion other than that the City of New York, acting through its agents, completely and negligently failed to fulfill this obligation to Linda.

***

The instant case provides an excellent illustration of the limits which the courts can draw. No one would claim that, under the facts here, the police were negligent when they did not give Linda protection after her first calls or visits to the police station in February of 1959. The preliminary investigation was sufficient. If Linda had been attacked at this point, clearly there would be no liability here. When, however, as time went on and it was established that Linda was a reputable person, that other verifiable attempts to injure her or intimidate her had taken place, that other witnesses were available to support her claim that her life was being threatened, something more was required—either by way of further investigation or protection—than the statement that was made by one detective to Linda that she would have to be hurt before the police could do anything for her.

***

De Long v. Erie County

from *De Long v. Erie County,* 60 NY 2d 296 (1983)

In this suit for damages brought by the family and estate of a woman killed by a burglar, a jury found the City of Buffalo and the County of Erie liable for negligent processing of and response to the victim's call for emergency assistance made on the special 911 number established and serviced by the defendants.

***

In October, 1976 the decedent, Amalia De Long, resided with her husband and three small children in Kenmore, a village adjacent to the City of Buffalo. Her home at 319 Victoria Boulevard was located approximately 1,300 feet from the Kenmore Police Department. One of her neighbors was a captain in that department.

On the morning of October 25 she telephoned for emergency police assistance by dialing 911. At 9:29 her call was answered by a complaint writer employed by Erie County to respond to such requests. The call, lasting approximately 14 seconds, was recorded in its entirety as follows:

Caller: "Police?"

Complaint Writer: "911."

Caller: "Police, please come, 319 Victoria right away."

Complaint Writer: "What's wrong?"

***

Caller: "I heard a burglar; I saw his face in the back; he was trying to break in the house; please come right away."

Complaint Writer: "Okay, right away."

Caller: "Okay."

The complaint writer erroneously reported the address as 219 Victoria, and mistakenly assumed that the call had originated in Buffalo because he knew there was a Victoria Avenue in the city. Accordingly, after stamping the complaint card "flash" to indicate its high priority, he placed it on a conveyor belt which ran through a glass partition to the radio dispatcher for the Buffalo Police Department. At 9:30 the dispatcher broadcast a report of a burglary in progress to patrol cars in the vicinity of Victoria Avenue in the city. Three minutes later the officers who had responded to the call informed the dispatcher that there was no such address and that the highest number on Victoria was 195. At 9:34 the dispatcher "cleared the call", in effect telling the officers at the scene to disregard it. The dispatcher himself took no further action on the call.

At approximately 9:42 Mrs. De Long was seen running from her house, unclothed and bleeding profusely. She collapsed on the sidewalk in front of her home. A neighbor called the Kenmore Police and within a minute a police car responded — a few minutes later paramedics arrived. However by 9:53 she displayed no vital signs. An autopsy revealed that she had been stabbed several times and had died from loss of blood.

After filing a notice of claim against the city and the county, the decedent's husband commenced an action seeking damages for wrongful death and conscious pain and suffering.

At the trial it was shown that prior to 1975 the City of Buffalo had adopted the 911 number as the one to call for emergency services, including police and fire protection. At that time a person dialing the number within the city would immediately be connected with the Buffalo Police Department where a complaint writer would take the information and give it to a radio dispatcher who in turn would contact the appropriate patrol cars or other emergency vehicles. The complaint writers, originally police officers and later mostly civilians, together with the dispatchers were trained and supervised by a lieutenant or acting lieutenant from the Buffalo Police Department. In March of 1975 Erie County formed a new agency known as Central Police Services which took over the complaint writing function from the city and extended the 911 service to several communities beyond the city limits, including the Village of Kenmore. Thus in 1975 and 1976 the telephone directory for Erie County listed 911 as the emergency number for the "local police".

Under the system adopted by the county, however, a 911 call made within the City of Buffalo or the extended area would not automatically connect the caller with the police department servicing the caller's area. Instead the call would go to the Center for Emergency Services which, pursuant to an agreement with the city, was located in the old 911 room in the Buffalo Police Department headquarters. The stated purpose of the center was to "accept telephone requests for emergency services for all Public Safety Agencies within the service area of the Center, and relay, transfer, or forward such requests to the Public Safety Agency concerned, without requiring the caller to re-dial another telephone number." At this center the county employed its own complaint writers many of whom, including the one who answered the call in this case, had held the same position with the city. In accordance with the agreement the city was required to provide training, supervision and assistance to the complaint writers for a year or more and was still doing so in October, 1976. A Buffalo police lieutenant or acting lieutenant remained in the room to coordinate the activities of the complaint writers and Buffalo police dispatchers and to furnish assistance of a supervisory nature when necessary.

Most of the procedures previously followed by the city were adopted by the county and incorporated in the "Manual for 911 Services". The major additional requirement 303*303 imposed by the county was that the complaint writers obtain information concerning the location or municipality involved so that the complaint could be forwarded to the police department or other emergency service responsible for that area. This was the subject of additional training for those complaint writers who had previously been employed by the city. They were further instructed to determine the origin of the call at the outset because calls from the city were necessarily processed differently from those originating elsewhere. In the case of city calls the complaint card was placed on a conveyor belt which ran to the Buffalo police dispatcher's office in the room next to the center. For the noncity calls, buttons were installed at the complaint writer's desk which permitted him to immediately transfer the call to the appropriate agency and monitor it to insure that the connection had been made and that the call had been properly routed.

There was also a standard operating procedure for cases in which officers responding to the scene of a priority complaint reported "no such address". In that event the dispatcher was required to notify the lieutenant in charge or the complaint writer. They in turn would either replay the recording of the call to check the information or consult one of the street directories or "duplicate street" listings available at the center to determine whether the address provided could be located in another community.

The transcript of the recording and the testimony of various witnesses connected with the center showed that the complaint writer had failed to comply with the applicable regulations in several respects. He had neglected to obtain (1) the caller's name, (2) the complete street address which would have indicated Victoria Boulevard and not Victoria Avenue as he assumed and (3) the name of the locality or municipality where the call originated. He also neglected to verify the information by repeating it.

In addition, the police dispatcher completely neglected to initiate the follow-up procedures. He had not notified the lieutenant in charge or the complaint writer that the investigating officers could find no such address. He had simply disregarded the call because he assumed it was a "fake".

* * *

Under similar circumstances it has been held that a special relationship was created so as to require the municipality to exercise ordinary care in the performance of a duty it has voluntarily assumed. Thus a city may be held liable for neglecting to provide crossing guards for school children when it has voluntarily undertaken the task which the children's parents could justifiably expect to be regularly and properly performed (*Florence v Goldberg*, supra). Similarly a municipality which has affirmatively certified a building as safe may be held liable to the owners for injury caused by known, blatant and dangerous violations (*Garrett v Holiday Inns, supra;* but also see *O'Connor v City of New York*, 58 N.Y.2d 184). The basic principle, as Judge CARDOZO observed, is this: "If conduct has gone forward to such a stage that inaction would commonly result, not negatively merely in withholding a benefit, but positively or actively in working an injury, there exists a relation out of which arises a duty to go forward" (*Moch Co. v Rensselaer Water Co., 247 N.Y. 160, 167*; see, also, *Zibbon v Town of Cheektowaga*, 51 AD2d 448, app dsmd 39 N.Y.2d 1056).

***

CRITIQUING A STUDENT'S ARGUMENT

The following essay excerpt was written in response to the following question: After reading the cases of *Riss v. City of New York* (page 140) and *De Long v. Erie County* (page 141), write an essay arguing for or against a citizen's ability to sue a police department for negligence when a request for help is not granted.

In reviewing the excerpt that follows, look for a number of areas that need improvement: thesis statement problems, sentences that do not belong where they are (problems with unity or organization), logical fallacies, areas that need more expansion/detail, mistakes in integration of quotes, and run-ons.

Student Argument against Suing Police for Negligence

In 1968, there was a lawsuit against the City of New York, Linda Riss, a young woman, was the one who filed it. She was angry about police negligence and felt they should have given her better protection. She lost her suit. This may seem unfair at first, but the result was necessary. A person should not be able to sue the police just because they failed to give protection because it is impossible for police to protect everyone, and police should be entitled to use their professional judgment without getting sued for every bad outcome.

We live in a frightening world. As if street crime were not enough, there is always the threat of war or financial collapse. Sometimes it seems that every phone call brings bad news. Allowing a law suit every time the police refuse to protect a victim who needed protection might be fine if there were enough officers to protect everyone, but this is not the case. "A crime is committed every three seconds." "One out of every seven people will be the victim of a violent crime this year." Not every person who seeks protection from the police has a legitimate story. Many people who come in ask for protection or a restraining order have ridiculous stories to tell. Sometimes people have good stories but they turn out to be false, this can lead to very bad outcomes if the police believe them and take action. Police are not miracle workers and do not have enough time in the day to work on their current duties let alone take on new requests for help. I know firsthand how much of police resources are needed to give protection because I once needed that service myself and saw what was involved. There is no way that our police force, which consists of 342 full-time officers with a projected growth rate of 2% per year, can help more than a few people at a time. Our society either has to get better at solving its own problems without police, or else stop complaining when the police are not able to help.

Someone has to decide which will be the few people who receive help, and it is impossible to get it right every time. However, police do not just make random decisions. They get special training on who to believe. There was a famous case last year about a big liar who swore he needed protection. The chief of police had said: "We cannot help you." Obviously, in this case the police were right since the man was lying. Sometimes people lie just to get attention because there is something missing from the rest of their lives. They try to make themselves appear more interesting, but this only drives people farther away from them. There have also been situations where police helped citizens who didn't really need protection and ended up causing more problems. Therefore, the solution cannot just be to help everyone who asks for it.

Conciseness
The Crime of Attempt · Accomplice Liability

CONCISENESS

What is conciseness?

In one particular aspect, the writing style of some individuals tends to get worse as they get farther along in their education. Pressured into thinking that their writing will not sound professional, academic, or impressive enough, they try to emulate the bloated, pompous, convoluted sentences that run rampant in the business and legal worlds. This is a sickness that has spread throughout our society. Clear, straightforward expression is devalued. People actually strive to create texts that will consume more paper, require more time to read, communicate less clarity, and generate more confusion. It is vital to combat this plague by learning to make your own writing sleek, streamlined, and direct. The art of using only the words necessary for the desired effect is called *conciseness.*

Why do students resist conciseness?

In addition to the motivations just described, there is another reason many students are reluctant to trim down their sentences in pursuit of conciseness: word count. Almost all writing assignments in college specify a minimum page or word count, so desperate students scramble to find longer ways to say what they've already said, compulsively running a word count after every line to see if they are approaching their long-desired goal.

This is self-defeating in two senses. Word counts are assigned because they are an instructor's best estimate to how long it should take to perform a writing task successfully. Adding filler to your paper doesn't take you any closer to your goal; it doesn't add evidence or subdivide the question any further. Secondly, instead of helping the paper, they are actually hurting it. The preposterously wordy sentences only add another weakness to the paper so that now instead of just underdeveloped it is both underdeveloped and poorly written.

If your essay is too short, the answer doesn't lie in inflating the sentences but in gathering more evidence and possibly in subdividing the question further (see page 44).

So too much detail is bad?

No, this is a common misinterpretation that students take away from a lesson on conciseness. The goal here is never to eliminate details or anything meaningful just to save words. If an ex-husband's behavior has been "irresponsible, selfish, and dangerous," we should by no means delete any of those words. They all describe separate things, and if we have multiple examples of each we will probably want them. Conciseness, as we shall see, has to do with eliminating words that ***add nothing*** to a sentence.

Principles of conciseness

Achieving a concise writing style takes practice. Perhaps the best way to start on this road is to survey a variety of different techniques for targeting unnecessary words. Most likely, you will find some of these techniques easier to apply than others. It would be useless to tell you to keep ***all*** of them in mind as you write and revise, but as you master more and more of them, the others will probably fall into place naturally.

Relocate modifiers that can become briefer when moved to the other side of the word they modify

Teachers *who have experience* know how to handle students *who generate problems.*	*Experienced* teachers know how to handle *problematic* students.
Acting in a manner that showed his foolishness, the executive forgot to burn the letter.	The executive *foolishly* forgot to burn the letter.

Strike words that mean nothing

~~As a matter of fact,~~ only four countries prohibit loitering.
~~What I want to say is that~~ we must resolve this issue.

Strike redundancies

We should learn from ~~past~~ history to avoid adding ~~additional~~ mistakes.
The folder containing the ~~verifying~~ proof was green ~~in color~~, which was ~~an unexpected~~ surprise.

Avoid starting with "There is/ There are"

There are four files *that* are *placed* on the table.	Four files are on the table.
There is a concept called "constructive eviction" *that applies to* this case.	This case involves constructive eviction.

Save words by combining related sentences

A man should *respect* his wife. When *respect* is lacking, the marriage's stability falls apart.	A man should respect his wife or expect the marriage's stability to fall apart.
After 40 hours, an employer must pay *overtime. Overtime* must be paid at a rate of time-and-a-half.	After 40 hours, an employer must pay time-and-a-half for overtime.

Eliminate tedious fanfare

~~After careful consideration, I have come to the conclusion that~~ this law is unjust.
~~At this point it seems fair to say that I think we should make the following observations~~.

Try to reword with fewer prepositional phrases

This card that is designed *for students to save money by riding the bus* is blue.	The money-saving student bus card is blue.
The representative of students gave a concert *at* noon for *the purpose of having* fun.	The student representative gave a noon concert for fun.

Turn nouns into verbs wherever possible

We will make a *plan* to have *dinner* and perform the *installation* of the software.	We will *plan* to *dine* and *install* the software.
If you go do the *drive* on Sunday, it can allow *relaxation* and provide *entertainment* for the family.	If you *drive* on Sunday, you can *relax* and *entertain* the family.

Avoid the passive voice

Your transaction *was unable to be* processed when an internal systems error *was experienced* by us.	We *committed* an error with your transaction.
A rise in fatalities *is* the probable consequence of our decision.	Our decision will probably *cost* lives.

More on the passive voice

Eliminating the passive voice is such an important step toward improving the clarity and conciseness of your writing that it warrants a few extra words. The passive voice arises when we write with passive verbs, such as *be, is, am, are, was,* and *were.* They are called passive because, unlike other verbs, they do not evoke any idea of activity. They just "are." Why are they bad? There are at least three reasons:

1. They are dull words that consume space a more interesting, specific verb could use, one that actually evokes a mental picture.

2. They tend to require that the actor, the "star" of the sentence, be taken away from the head of the sentence and buried farther in the back: *The president ordered a series of budget reviews* becomes *A series of budget reviews were ordered by the president.*

3. They almost always require extra prepositions and articles, which adds filler to the word count. Compare *We had dinner* with *A dinner was had by us.*

Very occasionally, the passive voice will work better than the active voice; for example, if you want to hide or deemphasize the actor of the sentence. In general, however, you will make your writing clearer and more engaging if you consistently choose the active voice. Target passive verbs and rephrase to eliminate them.

Practice with conciseness

Revise the following sentences, keeping all detail but using the strategies of conciseness presented.

Original	Revised for Conciseness
In the event that the police fail to follow the prescribed regulations that deal with matters of constitutional rights, the preferred response is to preserve this information in the file and advise the parties who may be involved that we have the intention to draw attention to the matter.	
Subsequent to learning of the existence of a complaint, the agent who is supervising expressed a desire that forces charged with the fighting of crime be dispatched to the site in order to effectuate a solution for the situation.	
The assault produced an impact of fear upon the victims who felt an onset of panic and initiated a series of screams.	
I made a note of the fact that the vehicle which was used for purposes of escape departed with a high velocity estimated to be in excess of 50 mph, and I made written notations as to the license plate for the future purpose of determining the occupant's identity.	
The point I would like to make is that the garbage, which was decaying, was picked up by me, but a promise was made by the landlord, who we rent from, that there is no need for the garbage to be picked up by us.	

A JUDICIAL OPINION

Assignment Memo

We believe that the judicial opinion that follows may be important for a case we are working on. As you may know, when an appeals court believes that a lower court committed errors in its handling of a case, it has the power to reverse their ruling. They then write a judicial opinion explaining why they do or do not believe that the lower court proceeded appropriately.

The opinion reverses a lower court who had found John Hicks guilty as an accomplice to the murder of Andrew J. Colvard. The lower court had felt that Hicks contributed to the killing of Colvard by laughing and saying words that encouraged Stand Rowe to shoot Colvard. In the opinion, the U.S. Supreme Court disagrees and lists a number of errors that the lower judge made when he gave the jury guidelines for how to make their decision. According to the Supreme Court, using these flawed guidelines, the jury could not have returned a fair verdict. Please do the following:

1. Revise the opinion by keeping all the important details but making it more concise. I have highlighted sentences that are in special need of revising. Aim to reduce the whole passage from 2,348 words to about 1,550 words.

2. Identify any logical fallacies that you see in the lower judge's way of thinking, using the terms on page 108 wherever possible.

from *Hicks v. United States*, 150 U.S. 442 (1893)

***

"It appears that on the night of the 12th of February, 1892, there was a dance at the house of Jim Rowe, in the Cherokee Nation; that Jim Rowe was a brother to Stand Rowe, who was indicted jointly with the defendant; that a large number of men and women were in attendance; that the dance continued until near sunrise the morning of the 13th; that Stand Rowe and the defendant were engaged in what was called 'scouting,' viz., eluding the United States marshals who were in search of them with warrants for their arrest, and were armed for the purpose of resisting arrest; they appeared at the dance, each armed with a Winchester rifle; they were both Cherokee Indians. The deceased, Andrew J. Colvard, was a white man who had married a Cherokee woman; he had been engaged in the mercantile business in the Cherokee country until a few months before the homicide; he came to the dance on horseback on the evening of the 12th. A good deal of whiskey was drank during the night by the persons present, and Colvard appears to have been drunk at some time during the night. Colvard spoke Cherokee fluently, and appears to have been very friendly with Stand Rowe and the defendant Hicks.

***

"Some time after sunrise on the morning of the 13th, about 7 o'clock, S.J. Christian, Benjamin F. Christian, Wm. J. Murphy, and Robert Murphy, all of whom had been at the dance the night before and had seen there Colvard, Stand Rowe, and the defendant, were standing on the porch of the house of William J. Murphy, about 414 steps west from the house of Jim Rowe, and saw Stand Rowe, coming on horseback in a moderate walk, with his Winchester rifle lying down in front of him, down a 'trail,' which led into the main travelled road. ***

"As Colvard and Hicks approached the point where Stand Rowe was sitting on his horse, Stand Rowe rode out into the road and halted. Colvard then rode up to him in a lope or canter, leaving Hicks, the defendant, some 30 or 40 feet in his rear. The point where the three men were together on their horses was about 100 yards from where the four witnesses stood on the porch. The conversation between the three men on horseback was not fully heard by the four men on the porch, and all that was heard was not understood, because part of it was carried on in the Cherokee tongue; but some part of this conversation was distinctly heard and clearly understood by these witnesses; they saw Stand Rowe twice raise his rifle and aim it at Colvard, and twice he lowered it; they heard Colvard say, 'I am a friend to both of you;' they saw and heard the defendant Hicks laugh aloud when Rowe directed his rifle toward Colvard; they saw Hicks take off his hat and hit his horse on the neck or shoulder with it; they heard Hicks say to Colvard, 'Take off your hat and die like a man;' they saw Stand Rowe raise his rifle for the third time, point it at Colvard, fire it; they saw Colvard's horse wheel and run back in the direction of Jim Rowe's house, 115 or 116 steps; they saw Colvard fall from his horse; they went to where he was lying in the road and found him dead; they saw Stand Rowe and John Hicks ride off together after the shooting."

Hicks testified in his own behalf, denying that he had encouraged Rowe to shoot Colvard, and alleging that he had endeavored to persuade Rowe not to shoot.

At the trial the government's evidence clearly disclosed that John Hicks, the accused, did not, as charged in the indictment, shoot the deceased, nor take any part in the physical struggle. To secure a conviction it hence became necessary to claim that the evidence showed such participation in the felonious shooting of the deceased as to make the accused an accessory, or that he so acted in aiding and abetting Rowe as to make him guilty as a principal. ***

The language attributed to Hicks, and which he denied having used, cannot be said to have been entirely free from ambiguity. It was addressed not to Rowe, but to Colvard.

Hicks testified that Rowe was in a dangerous mood, and that he did not know whether he would shoot Colvard or Hicks. The remark made — if made — accompanied with the gesture of taking off his own hat, may have been an utterance of desperation, occasioned by his belief that Rowe would shoot one or both of them. That Hicks and Rowe rode off together after seeing Colvard fall was used as a fact against Hicks, pointing to a conspiracy between them. Hicks testified that he did it in fear of his life; that Rowe had demanded that he should show him the road which he wished to travel. Hicks further testified, and in this he was not contradicted, that he separated from Rowe a few minutes afterwards, on the first opportunity, and that he never afterwards had any intercourse with him, nor had he been in the company of Rowe for several weeks before the night of the fatal occurrence.

Two of the assignments of error are especially relied on by the counsel of the accused. One arises out of that portion of the charge wherein the judge sought to instruct the jury as to the evidence relied on as showing that Hicks aided and abetted Rowe in the commission of the crime. The language of the learned judge was as follows:

"We are to proceed then to see whether the defendant was a party to the killing — that is, whether he was connected with it, or so aided or assisted in producing the act, as under the law he is responsible by the rules of the law for that act, as well as the man who fired the fatal shot if he were alive. We go to the first proposition where the crime of murder has been committed, which asserts that he who with his own hand did the act which produced the result is guilty. The second proposition is, that if at the time that Andrew J. Colvard was shot by Stand Rowe, the defendant was present at that time and at the place of shooting, that, of course, would not alone make him guilty — the mere fact that he was present. *** If the defendant was actually or constructively present at that time, and in any way aided or abetted by word or by advising or encouraging the shooting of Colvard by Stand Rowe *** he is made a participant in the crime as thoroughly and completely as though he had with his own hand fired the shot which took the life of the man killed. That is the second condition. The law further says that if he was actually present at that place at the time of the firing by Stand Rowe, and he was there for the purpose of either aiding, abetting, advising, or encouraging the shooting of Andrew J. Colvard by Stand Rowe, and that as a matter of fact he did not do it, but was present at the place for the purpose of aiding or abetting or advising or encouraging his shooting, but he did not do it because it was not necessary, it was done without his assistance, the law says there is a third condition where guilt is fastened to his act in that regard."

We agree with the counsel for the plaintiff in error in thinking that this instruction was erroneous in two particulars. It omitted to instruct the jury that the acts or words of encouragement and abetting must have been used by the accused with the intention of encouraging and abetting Rowe. So far as the instruction goes, the words may have been used for a different purpose, and yet have had the actual effect of inciting Rowe to commit the murderous act. Hicks, indeed, testified that the expressions used by him were intended to dissuade Rowe from shooting. But the jury were left to find Hicks guilty as a principal because the effect of his words may have had the result of encouraging Rowe to shoot, regardless of Hicks' intention. ***

Another error is contained in that portion of the charge now under review, and that is the statement "that if Hicks was actually present at that place at the time of the firing by Stand Rowe, and he was there for the purpose of either aiding, abetting, advising, or encouraging the shooting of Andrew J. Colvard by Stand Rowe, and that, as a matter of fact, he did not do it, but was present for the purpose of aiding or abetting or advising or encouraging his shooting but he did not do it because it was not necessary, it was done without his assistance, the law says there is a third condition where guilt is fastened to his act in that regard."

We understand this language to mean that where an accomplice is present for the purpose of aiding and abetting in a murder, but refrains from so aiding and abetting because it turned out not to be necessary for the accomplishment of the common purpose, he is equally guilty as if he had actively participated by words or acts of encouragement. Thus understood, the statement might, in some instances, be a correct instruction. Thus, if there had been evidence sufficient to show that there had been a previous conspiracy between Rowe and Hicks to waylay and kill Colvard, Hicks, if present at the time of the killing, would be guilty, even if it was found unnecessary for him to act. But the error of such an instruction, in the present case, is in the fact that there was no evidence on which to base it. The evidence *** shows no facts from which the jury could have properly found that the rencounter was the result of any previous conspiracy or arrangement. ***

Another assignment seems to us to present a substantial error. This has to do with the instructions by the learned judge to the jury, on the weight which they should give to the testimony of the accused in his own behalf. Those instructions were in the following words:

"The defendant has gone upon the stand in this case and made his statement. You are to weigh its reasonableness, its probability, its consistency, and above all you consider it in the light of the other evidence, in the light of the other facts. If he is contradicted by other reliable facts, that goes against him, goes against his evidence. You may explain it perhaps on the theory of an honest mistake or a case of forgetfulness, but if there is a conflict as to material facts between his statements and the statements of the other witnesses who are telling the truth, then you would have a contradiction that would weigh against the statements of the defendant as coming from such witnesses. You are to consider his interest in this case; you are to consider his consequent motive growing out of that interest in passing upon the truthfulness or falsity of his statement. He is in an attitude, of course, where any of us, if so situated, would have a large interest in the result of the case, the largest, perhaps, we could have under any circumstances in life, and such an interest, consequently, as might cause us to make statements to influence a jury in passing upon our case that would not be governed by the truth; we might be led away from the truth because of our desire. Therefore it is but right, and it is your duty to view the statements of such a witness in the light of his attitude and in the light of other evidence."

***

The obvious objection to this suggestion is in its assumption that the other witnesses, whose statements contradicted those of the accused, were "telling the truth."

***

It is not easy to say what effect this instruction had upon the jury. If this were the only objectionable language contained in the charge, we might hesitate in saying that it amounted to reversible error. It is not unusual to warn juries that they should be careful in giving effect to the testimony of accomplices; and, perhaps, a judge cannot be considered as going out of his province in giving a similar caution as to the testimony of the accused person. Still it must be remembered that men may testify truthfully, although their lives hang in the balance, and that the law, in its wisdom, has provided that the accused shall have the right to testify in his own behalf. Such a privilege would be a vain one if the judge, to whose lightest word the jury, properly enough, give a great weight, should intimate that the dreadful condition in which the accused finds himself should deprive his testimony of probability. The wise and humane provision of the law is that "the person charged shall, at his own request, but not otherwise, be a *competent* witness." The policy of this enactment should not be defeated by hostile comments of the trial judge, whose duty it is to give reasonable effect and force to the law.

These strictures cannot be regarded as inappropriate when the facts of the present case are considered. The only substantial evidence against the accused, on which the jury had a right to find him guilty, was that of witnesses who testified to words used by him at a distance of not less than one hundred yards. Apart from the language so attributed to him, there was no evidence that would have warranted a jury in condemning him. His denial of his use of the words and his explanation of his conduct should, we think, have been submitted to the jury as entitled to the most careful consideration.

***

The judgment of the court below is
Reversed and the cause remanded, with directions to set aside the verdict and award a new trial.

WRITING TASKS: ACCOMPLICE LIABILITY

From studying the *Hicks* case, we can articulate the following criteria as our definition of ***accomplice liability***—that is, the act of assisting someone else to commit a crime.

The Elements of Accomplice Liability

1. The defendant must have aided, abetted, counseled, or incited the crime, either through an action or through failure to perform a duty required by law.

2. The defendant must have intended to aid, abet, counsel, or incite the crime.

3. The defendant must intend for the crime to occur.

Assignment Memo

Keeping in mind the rules for accomplice liability, consider the following two cases. In one, the defendant was found guilty, while in the other he was not. Unfortunately, we have lost the records telling us the outcomes of the cases. They are too expensive to reorder, so please write a comparison essay, explaining which defendant you believe should be charged as an accomplice and which should not. In terms of structure, you will want a task list like the following:

1. Introduce the concept of accomplice liability and briefly mention the cases.

2. Define accomplice liability precisely.

3. Compare the two cases and assign guilt where appropriate.

4. Conclude by explaining why the two cases ended with opposite results.

from *Pace v. State of Indiana*, 248 Ind. 146 (1967)

***

Viewing the evidence most favorable to the State, the record shows the following: appellant, his wife, and two infant children were in a car driving from South Bend to LaPorte. Eugene Rootes was riding with them. The appellant was driving with his wife and one child in the front seat. Rootes and appellant's other child were in the back seat. While in South Bend, appellant after asking his wife for permission stopped to pick up a hitchhiker, Mr. Reppert, who sat next to Rootes in the back seat with one of appellant's infant children. Later Rootes pulled a knife and took Reppert's wallet. After driving further, Reppert got out of the car, Rootes then took his watch. The appellant said nothing during the entire period and they continued driving to LaPorte. This is all of the evidence presented by the record which would have any bearing on the crime charged, (i.e., accessory before the fact of robbery by placing in fear).

***

END

from *Settles v. U.S.*, 522 A.2d 348 (DC: Court of Appeals, 1987)

***

At approximately 4:15 p.m. on April 17, 1984, a woman whom we shall call Gloria Smith (not her real name) was walking with her three-year-old son Kevin to her grandmother's house. *** As they passed the rear of an apartment complex, two men suddenly approached them from behind. One of the men—appellant Settles—put his hand over Smith's mouth and shoved her into the basement of a nearby apartment building. Kevin, who had been holding his mother's hand, followed her into the basement. *** Although Whitley did not go into the basement with the others, Smith testified that he stood "right outside of the door." When the prosecutor asked, "How do you know that?", she replied, "Because I saw him." On cross-examination Smith testified that Whitley was "about three or four feet, I guess," from the door.

Inside the basement, Settles struck Smith in the face and on the back of the head. When her young son began to cry, Settles told her to "shut that boy up" and pushed him in the chest, but he did not stop crying. *** Settles thereupon put his finger and then his penis into her vagina from behind, attempting to have sexual intercourse, while Kevin stood next to his mother holding her hand. After a short while Settles told Smith that he did not want to hurt her. Ordering her not to turn around, he walked over to the door and started to open it. *** Then he opened the door and went outside. When Smith went to the door and looked out, she saw Settles and Whitley running away together, side by side.

***

A RESEARCH TASK: ACCOMPLICE LIABILITY

Assignment Memo

If a person helps put someone in a position to commit a crime, does that always make the person an accomplice? After reading the facts of the following two cases, decide whether you would hold the defendants guilty as accomplices (Gladstone to the sale of drugs, Lauria to prostitution). Then do some research to find other examples of what we will call crime-enablers. You might look for people who bring clients to illegal performers of abortions, who coordinate sales of drugs between two others, or who bring clients to prostitutes. Were they found guilty? Should they have been? After researching the subject, write an essay based on a thesis that identifies guidelines to determine whether the enabler of a crime is charged as an accomplice.

from *State v. Gladstone*, 78 Wash. 2d 306 (1970)

***

Thompson testified that Lieutenant Seymour and Detective Gallwas of the narcotics detail asked him to attempt purchase of marijuana from Gladstone. During the evening of April 10, 1967—between 10 and 11 o'clock—the two officers and Thompson drove in a police car to the vicinity of defendant's apartment. Thompson went to Gladstone's door alone, beyond the hearing and out of the sight of the two officers. He knocked at the door and Gladstone responded. Thompson asked Gladstone if he would sell him some marijuana. Describing this incident, Thompson testified as follows:

Well, I asked—at the time Gladstone told me that he was—he did not have enough marijuana on hand to sell me any, but he did know an individual who had quite a sufficient quantity and that was very willing to sell and he named the individual as Robert Kent, or Bob Kent as he put it, and he gave me directions to the residence and he—due to the directions I asked him if, you know, if he could draw me a map and he did.

When Thompson said he asked Gladstone to draw the map for him, he added, "I'm not sure whether he did give me the exact address or not, he told me where the residence was." He said that Gladstone then with pencil and paper sketched the location of Kent's place of residence. Thompson had no prior knowledge of where Kent lived, and did not know if he might have marijuana or that he had ever possessed it.

The two officers then took Thompson to Kent's residence where marijuana was purchased. The actual purchase was made by Thompson directly from Kent while Officer Gallwas and Lieutenant Seymour stayed in the police car. Kent was subsequently arrested and convicted of selling Thompson approximately 8 ounces of marijuana—the very sale which defendant here was convicted of aiding and abetting.

from *People v. Lauria,* 251 Cal. App. 2d 471 (2nd Dist., 2nd Div. 1967)

***

In an investigation of call-girl activity the police focused their attention on three prostitutes actively plying their trade on call, each of whom was using Lauria's telephone answering service, presumably for business purposes.

On January 8, 1965, Stella Weeks, a policewoman, signed up for telephone service with Lauria's answering service. Mrs. Weeks, in the course of her conversation with Lauria's office manager, hinted broadly that she was a prostitute concerned with the secrecy of her activities and their concealment from the police. She was assured that the operation of the service was discreet and "about as safe as you can get." It was arranged that Mrs. Weeks need not leave her address with the answering service, but could pick up her calls and pay her bills in person.

On February 11, Mrs. Weeks talked to Lauria on the telephone and told him her business was modelling and she had been referred to the answering service by Terry, one of the three prostitutes under investigation. She complained that because of the operation of the service she had lost two valuable customers, referred to as tricks. Lauria defended his service and said that her friends had probably lied to her about having left calls for her. But he did not respond to Mrs. Weeks' hints that she needed customers in order to make money, other than to invite her to his house for a personal visit in order to get better acquainted. In the course of his talk he said "his business was taking messages."

***

On April 1 Lauria and the three prostitutes were arrested. *** When asked if his records were available to police who might come to the office to investigate call girls, Lauria replied that they were whenever the police had a specific name. However, his service didn't "arbitrarily tell the police about prostitutes on our board. As long as they pay their bills we tolerate them." In a subsequent voluntary appearance before the grand jury Lauria testified he had always cooperated with the police. But he admitted he knew some of his customers were prostitutes ***.

Essay Mechanics
Contracts

A PROBLEMATIC CONTRACT

Assignment Memo

Our client signed the following contract upon assuming a new position as manager at ABC Co. However, the more she studies the contract, the more confused she is becoming. After reading the contract, she took the following actions. First, ignoring all the offices in the western part of the city of Covina, she promptly told all the offices in West Covina that she was taking over. She told the owner of Superior Vendors to get lost and replaced them with agreements with other vendors that she felt were of higher quality. Then she checked the immigration status of all the employees and asked those who were lawfully employed to approve her raise negotiations. When asked why she did these strange things, she re-read the contract and realized just how ambiguous it is.

Using your knowledge of capitalization and punctuation, please identify every ambiguous element of the contract and advise her as to what course of action she should take regarding each element. You can find a summary of the relevant capitalization and punctuation rules following the contract.

Linda's Contract

Manager will have control over every office except those in west covina, and she will be expected to spend more than 50% of her time in the central office. Manager agrees to order supplies only from superior vendors. Before deciding to negotiate any raises, the final decision must be approved by the firms legal employees. None of the following are permitted on company grounds: Fundraising Party, gambling, smoking. Due to agreements with outside vendors, only scotch tape should be used within the office. Do not allow Idle Gossip to enter the workplace. Requests for alterations to this agreement must be submitted to your supervisors, Mr. Harris and Mrs. Smith. Exceptions to these terms can only be authorized by Father Garcia and James. When speaking with Steven Taylor James White should be notified. While you are working the street door should be open. Sometimes staff members have no daycare. Considering the problem children will be allowed. Lunch breaks over an hour are forbidden and noisy conversations should be discouraged. Please make sure that New's papers are always available for our customers. Priority should always be given to our customers phone calls and letters get second priority.

If our vice president calls, his wifes messages should be given to him immediately. Make sure that anyone receiving a good driver discount is driving a Passenger Vehicle. During the last three years to qualify a driver must not have a DUI accident resulting in injury or citation. Paper, water and other fluids for drinking must be paid for personally by Manager. Employees are to take turns watching the customers exit at closing time. Any request to leave early must be sent to Lukas and Kevin's secretaries.

Late employees who irritate the manager shall be dismissed after the third infraction. Any free time should be spent watching the customers cleaning the floors and studying the employee manual. Employees who are not moving the products will be replaced by personnel in blue shirts who are newly hired and fired. Anyone who disrupts The Office will be immediately dismissed. Employees are not to bring their friend's, children, or pets into the business. All employees must wear an apron with a picture of a red hot dog. The Manager is the one who plans shifts and turns. After everyone leaves the store the parking lot and the reception area and the front door should be thoroughly cleaned. This contract will continue for five years, and there will be no raises unless after the last sale of the term it is found that the sales volume is higher than the stores average.

CAPITALIZATION

The rules are numerous and sometimes debatable. However, you will do well to master the one basic concept that explains 90% of uncertainties: Capitalize a word only if it is an official name intended to represent someone's or something's unique identity.

Thus, when people in the United States speak of "the South," they are referring to a specific region that has come to acquire "the South" as its name. However, the southeast portion of the United States is not commonly known by any such name, so "southeast" is merely a description, not a name. As another example, if I ask you about your grandmother, I will not capitalize "grandmother" because, for me, that is not her name.

But when you say, "Hello Grandmother," for you that *is* her name. That's what you call her, and if a word acts like a name then you capitalize it like a name. When you refer to Kleenex^{TM}, you need to capitalize because that is actually the name of a brand. Alternatively, you could refer to tissue. When talking about any old civil war, that is different from using an official name, such as the Spanish Civil War. Since there is no nation called "White," it is correct to refer to white people, but Chinese citizens. You would ask about your boss, but if you call him Boss Henry, then bring out the capital "B." The title of the South Beach Book Club contains four words, but the South Beach book club is just an unnamed book club that happens to be in South Beach. We capitalize month names and days of the week because their names derive from mythical and historical figures, but we don't capitalize the four seasons because they are not named after anyone (although we do capitalize The Four Seasons if it is the name of a band, movie, or musical composition).

Most of the other rules are just conventions, which means you memorize them and don't ask why. Always capitalize the following: 1) the word "I"; 2) the first word of a sentence; 3) the major words of a title; and 4) initials, such as Albert T. Smith or the CIA.

When in doubt, the Internet has thousands of exhaustive guides on the matter.

COMMAS

The comma is the most misused punctuation mark, no doubt because there are so many different rules governing its use. When a comma isn't required according to one rule, another rule may call for it. To top it all off, sometimes we use a comma in defiance of all the rules for the general reason that it avoids confusion. This is itself confusing.

Mastering five rules will set you right 90% of the time. If you find yourself wanting to include a comma in a situation that doesn't match one of the following five rules, the chances are that it should not be used.

Comma rule #1: lists

Use a comma to separate more than two items (nouns) in a list or a series of descriptive words (adjectives). However, if you have descriptive words that cannot be rearranged in a different order, they generally should NOT be separated by a comma.

Examples of Comma Rule #1

The contraband included guns, drugs, and alcohol.
The dark, stuffy hideout was full of clues.

BUT

They attacked a little old lady.

Because you would probably not rearrange the descriptive words to read …

They attacked an old little lady.

Comma rule #2: introductory words

If a sentence starts with an introductory phrase or clause instead of with its true subject, the person or thing that is performing the main action of the sentence, put a comma just before the true subject. If the true subject comes at the beginning of the sentence, this rule will not come into play. In the examples that follow, each sentence's subject is marked with ***bold italics.***

Examples of Comma Rule #2

After the arrest, ***the police*** found the contraband. During the getaway, ***they*** lost it. Because it was crucial, ***they*** looked for it.

BUT

The police found the contraband after the arrest. ***They*** lost it during the getaway. ***They*** looked for it because it was crucial.

Comma rule #3: joining independent clauses

Two independent clauses can be joined with a comma plus a conjunction, such as "and," "but," or "or." See page 69 for more on independent clauses and page 73 for more on joining them together. Note that when two clauses joined together with a conjunction are NOT both independent clauses, a comma should NOT be used. The test is this: do both clauses on either side of the conjunction (marked below in ***bold italics***) make sense by themselves? If so, a comma goes before the conjunction.

Examples of Comma Rule #3

The police made the arrest, ***and*** the chief found the contraband. The criminals escaped, ***and*** the evidence was lost. They needed to find it, ***so*** they looked for it.

BUT

The police made the arrest ***and*** made sure it was correct. The criminals escaped ***and*** stole a car. They needed to find it ***but*** could not.

Comma rule #4: interrupting a sentence

Sometimes a sentence is interrupted, either to add emphasis or to add extra detail that doesn't really change the meaning. If words could be removed from the sentence without losing the same basic message, put commas on both sides of the interrupting material.

Examples of Comma Rule #4

Officer Smith, ***known for his excellence***, made the arrest. Prisoner #463, ***however***, escaped. This led, ***unfortunately***, to the contraband being lost. Officer Smith, ***who was responsible***, looked desperately for it.

BUT

The officer ***who first saw the incident*** made the arrest. The criminals ***that robbed the store*** escaped. This led to a chase ***in which the contraband was lost***. The officer ***who was responsible*** looked desperately for it.

Comma rule #5: miscellaneous conventions

Some uses of the comma are just around by tradition. We use a comma to separate city names from state names, people's names from their titles,

between an announced quotation and its lead-in (see page 85), and PG#?
between the elements of a written number.

Examples of Comma Rule #5

Officer Smith comes from Columbus, Ohio and has worked for the city for one thousand, two hundred, and sixty-three days. On this subject he says, "It's been a great time." He says that he hopes one day to become just like his mentor John Stone, Commissioner of Police.

APOSTROPHES

For years, a debate has raged between punctuation lobbyists who think the apostrophe is useless and should be abolished and those who defend it. By most standards, however, it remains true that misusing the apostrophe will drastically undercut your credibility and interfere with clarity. Most students know how to use the apostrophe in contractions, so we will focus on its other important use, to signal a possessive.

As if apostrophes weren't mired in enough controversy already, there is some disagreement on exactly how the rules apply. You will do well to remember one basic principle:

Apostrophe Use

To show ownership, place the apostrophe so that the owner appears to its left.

John's book	The book belongs to John.
James's book	The book belongs to James.
The neighbors' dog	The dog belongs to more than one neighbor.
The neighbor's dog	The dog belongs to one neighbor.
The children's dog	The dog belongs to the children.
Sally and Tom's houses	The houses belong to Sally and Tom together.
Sally's and *Tom's* houses	One or more houses belong to Sally only, and one or more houses belong to Tom only.

One other rule should be mentioned:

Apostrophe Misuse

Do not use an apostrophe to mark a plural. **Exception**: to mark the plural of digits or letters.

Examples: There are two i's in "religious." There are four 5's in her phone number.

BUT

The Smiths are coming over to dinner. There are four ATMs on this street.

FORMAT

In addition to establishing rules about how to document sources, MLA also provides specifications of how papers should be formatted overall. Here are some of the most important highlights:

- Double-space throughout the paper. Do not skip extra lines between paragraphs.
- Begin each paragraph by indenting one tab stop to the right.
- Use 1-inch margins on all sides.
- Use a font of size 12. Times New Roman and Arial are good choices.
- Include your last name followed by a space, followed by the page number in the upper right corner of all pages and aligned to the right margin.
- At the top of the first page at the left margin, list your full name, your instructor's name, the course name, and the date—each on a separate line. Double-space these lines. Place the title of your paper two lines below the date, centered between the margins. Do not underline or italicize it, and do not use all capital letters.
- Be sure to secure all pages with a staple.

Sample MLA Format

John Doe

Professor Jung

English 15A

October 20, 2010

The Diva Under Theoretical Scrutiny

The fantasy of *To Wong Foo*, far from being an isolated idea, is wide-spread in contemporary popular culture. Most commonly, it appears under the rubric of "diva-worship": a cult-like fascination with female stars, with tributes ranging from avid (or rabid!) fan clubs to drag impersonators. As implied above, the myth of diva-worship claims an autonomous and liberating power available only to the female performer and—in considerably diluted form—to her imitators. Nor is this phenomenon unique to our period, evidence of similar attitudes and dialogues about the Diva being available throughout at least the past 100 years in both Britain and America. Precisely how and when this archetype emerges, and what nexus of cultural forces determines and sustains the Diva are the subjects of my investigation.

I focus on literary treatments of the female artist-performer, specifically the leading actress or opera singer, both of which I refer to with the term Diva. British literature in the final decades of the nineteenth century witnessed a proliferation of novels featuring this character type, a trend that I will argue reflects the convergence of changes in opera composition and production, the rise of the New Woman, and the Aesthetic Movement. My study of the genesis and representation of the Diva will engage questions important to any feminist archetypal criticism: how "useful" or positive is this archetype as a model of female power? What are the theoretical ramifications and implications of labeling a power as "feminine" and attributing it to this type?

Writing Practice

MURDER

Assignment Memo

Please review the laws pertaining to murder in the document below and write an essay determining what would happen if Mr. and Mrs. Macbess would be charged with murder. Specifically, your essay should answer the following questions: Will Mr. Macbess be found guilty of first- or second-degree murder, involuntary manslaughter, or nothing in the death of the King? What about in the death of Banquod? Will Mrs. Macbess be found guilty as an accomplice in the death of the king? What about in the death of Banquod?

In your essay, you should assume that all the facts given to you about the Macbess case are somehow discovered and presented to the jury and that the jury believes all of it. The purpose of your essay is to explain how the Rules of Murder will lead to the conviction or acquittal of these two persons for these two crimes.

Rules of Murder

Murder and Malice. A murder is the killing of one human by another with a mental frame of mind known as **malice aforethought.** This means that the first step in convicting a killer of murder is to prove that he had malice aforethought. This can be shown according to four different theories, and a prosecutor can show that a killer meets any or all of those criteria in case the defense is able to contradict one of them. Here are the four theories or routes by which a killer can be pinned with malice aforethought: 1) killer had the **intent to kill** or **knew for sure** that death would result (e.g., fires a gun at victim's head or puts a bomb on his plane); 2) killer had the **intent to cause serious**

physical harm or knew it would probably result (e.g., tries and wants to sever victim's finger); 3) killer showed ***reckless indifference to the value of human life*** (e.g., fires a gun into an apartment building for fun or drives 60 mph on a crowded sidewalk); or 4) killer intended to commit ***some other dangerous felony.*** This last is known as the felony murder rule and requires more explanation.

<u>Felony Murder Rule.</u> This refers to the fourth possibility for proving malice aforethought. The rule is that a killer who causes a death while in the progress of intentionally committing a dangerous felony is deemed to have acted with malice aforethought, even if the killing was accidental and never planned. Notice that even though it may be accidental, the death still has to be *caused* directly (proximately) by the killer's acts. An earthquake that kills a victim during a bank robbery will not count. The death must happen during the felony, which is considered to still be in progress until the killer has successfully completed the escape. The death could even occur before the felony itself as long as the plan for the felony had already been formed. Finally, the "triggering" felony has to be separate from the act of killing itself, or else all killings would be under this rule. The idea is that a death occurring while ***some other*** dangerous felony is in progress will trigger malice aforethought.

<u>Without malice, manslaughter may be possible.</u> If the prosecution cannot prove that the killer acted with malice, it may still be possible to charge involuntary manslaughter if it can be proven that the killer was ***grossly negligent.*** This would mean that the killer departed from the usual standards of care so substantially that he involuntarily exposed his victim to considerable and unjustified risk of harm.

<u>First vs. Second Degree Murder.</u> Getting back to murder, if murder is proven, it must be determined whether it is first degree or second degree. A murder is first degree if it can be shown that the killing was premeditated (planned out ahead of time). To prove that something was premeditated, it helps to identify evidence of 1) an elaborate plan; 2) a preexisting motive (a desire to inherit money as opposed to sudden anger); and 3) a method of killing that does not seem spontaneous (e.g., poisoning vs. shoving). Any murder that is not first degree is automatically second degree. But remember that if malice cannot be proven, there is no murder. There is either manslaughter or perhaps no crime at all.

<u>Accomplices.</u> The general rule is that one who aids or encourages another to commit a crime is guilty of the same crime. Even words may be enough if they help in some way, and assistance counts even if it turns out it wasn't necessary. If it turns out that the assistance was completely useless, though, that might be a defense. Just being present or just knowing about the crime is not enough. Assistance after the crime doesn't count, either. The prosecutor has to show that the alleged accomplice wanted the crime to happen, that the accomplice helped in the commission of the crime, and that the accomplice intended to help (as opposed to helping by accident).

Are accomplices liable for additional crimes? Sometimes the primary criminal commits further crimes beyond what the accomplice set out to assist. The accomplice will be guilty of all crimes that are natural, foreseeable consequences of the original crime even if the accomplice never intended them. However, if the primary criminal goes beyond the foreseeable and commits further crimes for personal or random motives, the accomplice will not be guilty of those.

But what if the killing happened unexpectedly? A defendant may try to argue that although he did something wrong, superseding causes came along and killed the victim. Without those superseding causes, the victim might not have died, so it is unfair to blame the death on the defendant. Will this argument work? It depends on the supposedly superseding cause. If death resulted directly from the defendant's actions, it won't matter if it happened in a slightly different way from what was intended. For example, if you intend to strike your victim a fatal blow, but you miss, and he has a heart attack and dies, it is still your fault. If some external factor gets in the way and slightly alters the result, it will still be your fault unless it is wildly coincidental. For example, if you intend to shoot your victim and hit him, it won't matter if his death happens from his refusal of medical care for religious reasons or from jumping out a window to get away. You are still the cause. Perhaps, if the gunshot wakens a rhinoceros who charges into the room and kills your victim, you might get off the hook.

The Case of the MacBess Murders

Mr. Macbess was a loyal warrior who was greatly trusted by his King. Simpleminded and content with his role in life, he was happy with his rather low position and never asked for more. However, Mrs. Macbess was fiercely ambitious and constantly pressured her husband to seek promotions and demand recognition for his abilities. As time went on, her pressuring increased and she began to insinuate that she might leave him if he did not improve his status in life.

One night, it happened that King was to spend the night at the Macbess mansion. After he arrived, Mrs. Macbess took her husband to one side. "This is the best opportunity you will ever have," she said. "If King dies tonight, you will be one of the top contenders for the throne."

"I may be a soldier, but I am not a murderer," answered her husband. "He's our guest here tonight. I know you want me to do this, but I don't think I can."

"You disgust me," replied Mrs. Macbess. "Obviously, you do not even deserve to be called a man, let alone a husband. Just show a little backbone. You can do this. I know you can. Besides, have I ever told you how attractive I find you when you take command?"

These suggestions went against everything Mr. Macbess believed in. At last, however, worn down by low self-esteem, his will was overcome by his wife. He entered King's bedroom with a sharpened dagger in hand. Even then, he did not expect to use it. Though he had agreed to follow his wife's direction to kill King, he privately intended to frighten King into swearing to name him as his successor. Mr. Macbess entered the darkened bedroom with the knife extended before him pointing outward. "I don't want to hurt you," he blurted out. Failing to see the riding boots that King had carelessly flung onto the floor, he tripped and fell forward with the outstretched dagger unfortunately plunging into King's heart. King died.

King's death was blamed on unknown assassins, and Mr. Macbess did come to take his place on the throne. However, only weeks later, Mr. Macbess began to have some disturbing conversations with his best friend, Banquod. It seems that Banquod found the whole affair suspicious and perhaps had even overheard the couple arguing on the night of the murder. Mrs. Macbess found her husband one day absorbed in thought and asked him what was wrong.

"I'm worried about the situation with Banquod," he said somewhat cryptically.

Seeming to understand his meaning, his wife asked, "What are we going to do about it? I'm here to help."

But no matter how many times she asked, Mr. Macbess never answered her. Instead, he formed his own plan. He hid a sword behind a tree in a clearing about a half-mile from his home and then told Banquod that they needed to walk down there for a private consultation. Without explaining his purposes to his wife, Mr. Macbess told her to offer Banquod a pair of shoes that he had sabotaged so that the laces would constantly undo themselves. Mrs. Macbess had no idea of thel nature of the shoes or the purpose of this request, but she obeyed, and Banquod accepted and put on the shoes.

When the two men arrived at the clearing in the woods, Macbess waited for Banquod to tie his shoe and then pulled out the hidden sword and decapitated him with a single blow. Meanwhile, Mrs. Macbess, guessing that the shoes might have been poisoned, burned the box they had come in to hide the evidence.

ATTEMPTS

The law punishes people for attempting a crime even if they do not succeed. The idea is that this will deter people from making such attempts and that a criminal should not escape punishment just because a plan fails. However, this can lead to injustice in at least two important ways. First, there is the question of whether the defendant **really was intending** to attempt a crime. Since no result occurred, a defendant could conceivably argue that appearances were deceiving or that a joke was intended. Secondly, even if there is intent, the question remains of whether the defendant *went far enough* in his plan. Punishing someone for a crime that has barely begun or that is still an idea amounts to punishing people for bad thoughts.

For these reasons, the general rule is that to convict someone of attempting a crime, the prosecution must prove that 1) the defendant intended to commit the crime, and 2) the defendant took a *substantial step* toward that goal.

Further complications arise when it turns out that the crime being attempted was actually impossible. Should that matter? Should a person be charged with attempted murder if he shoots an already dead body, thinking that it is alive? What if he tries to break into a house, gets confused in the dark, and mistakenly breaks into his own house? Is that an attempted break-in and punishable by law?

Practice with Attempt

Consider the following situations. Then decide which examples you think the law should punish and why you believe that is fair.

1.   Adams and Baker form a plan to order a pizza and then mug the deliverer. They order the pizza. The pizza never arrives because the restaurant closes due to fire, but the police find out about the plan. The police go to the Adams and Baker residence but find no evidence except for a hunting knife sitting on a shelf near the front door. Attempted assault?

2.   Cheswick decides that he wants to find his boss and strangle him to death. It turns out that he has the wrong apartment number, and so he wanders around the complex for two hours hoping to run into him. He never does. Attempted murder?

3.   Dixon, an undocumented alien, attempts to bribe a border official with a $100 bill. It turns out that the person he believed to be an inspections officer was a janitor. Attempted bribery?

4.   Eglantine believed she was meeting with thieves to buy what they had told her was a stolen television. It turns out that the thieves are police officers and that the television is not really stolen. Attempted purchase of stolen goods?

5.   Felix finds what he thinks is a pound of cocaine in the street and carries it home. It turns out it is only flour. Attempted possession of drugs?

6. Grace fires at what she thinks is her ex-boyfriend. It turns out to be a manikin. Attempted assault with a deadly weapon?

7. Humbert fires a gun in the air for fun, and it almost hits a passerby in the head. Attempted murder?

8. Isabel fires a gun at a passerby intending to miss by an inch and scare him. She does miss by an inch. Attempted murder?

9. Jones enters a backyard illegally and lights a match just as police apprehend him. He claims that the match was for lighting a cigarette, and he does have cigarettes on him. Attempted arson?

10. Larson accepts $500 from an undercover agent with the agreement that he will procure a prostitute for him. An hour later, he returns to the agent alone. Before he can say anything, he is arrested. Attempted procurement of prostitution?

11. Mabel, an adult, phones a 16-year-old boy and invites him to her house with the intention to have sexual relations with him. He does not arrive, but police intercept the call and arrest Mabel. Attempted statutory rape?

12. Nestor tries to shoot his roommate but fails because he did not realize that the gun was a toy. Attempted murder?

13. Superstitious Olga believes that pouring salt in front of her neighbor's doorway will kill her, and she pours salt in front of her doorway. The neighbor is not harmed. Attempted murder?

Assignment Memo

In the case that follows, the state's attempt to convict Smallwood of attempted murder was overturned. Read the facts, and then compare them with the cases of Hinkhouse and Haines. Write an essay comparing the cases and arguing why Smallwood should be found not guilty, while the others were found guilty.

---

from *Smallwood v. State*, 680 A. 2d 512 (Md: Court of Appeals, 1996)

On August 29, 1991, Dwight Ralph Smallwood was diagnosed as being infected with the Human Immunodeficiency Virus (HIV). According to medical records from the Prince George's County Detention Center, he had been informed of his HIV-positive status by

September 25, 1991. In February 1992, a social worker made Smallwood aware of the necessity of practicing "safe sex" in order to avoid transmitting the virus to his sexual partners, and in July 1993, Smallwood told health care providers at Children's Hospital that he had only one sexual partner and that they always used condoms. Smallwood again tested positive for HIV in February and March of 1994.

On September 26, 1993, Smallwood and an accomplice robbed a woman at gunpoint, and forced her into a grove of trees where each man alternately placed a gun to her head while the other one raped her. On September 28, 1993, Smallwood and an accomplice robbed a second woman at gunpoint and took her to a secluded location, where Smallwood inserted his penis into her with "slight penetration." On September 30, 1993, Smallwood and an accomplice robbed yet a third woman, also at gunpoint, and took her to a local school where she was forced to perform oral sex on Smallwood and was raped by him. In each of these episodes, Smallwood threatened to kill his victims if they did not cooperate or to return and shoot them if they reported his crimes. Smallwood did not wear a condom during any of these criminal episodes.

Based upon his attack on September 28, 1993, Smallwood was charged with, among other crimes, *** the attempted second-degree murder of each of his three victims.

***

from *State v. Hinkhouse*, 912 P.2d 921 (Or. Ct. App. 1996)

***

On November 3, 1990, defendant told his probation officer, Bill Carroll, that defendant was HIV-positive. Carroll immediately advised defendant of the implications of his HIV status, explaining the seriousness of the disease and the manner in which it is transmitted. Carroll explained that using a condom limits the risks of transmitting the virus, but he also explained that it would not eliminate the risk entirely. He told defendant that if he passed the virus to another person, "he would be killing someone." ***

Nevertheless, defendant continued to engage in sexual relations with a number of women. When he was taken into custody again for another probation violation later that year, he was heard bragging about his sexual prowess with women, expressing neither concern nor remorse for the people whom he might have exposed to HIV. As a condition of his release, however, he signed a probation agreement that included a commitment not to engage in any unsupervised contact with women without express permission from his parole officer.

In 1993, defendant began several sexual relationships without notifying Carroll. In each case, he refused to use a condom during sex and failed to disclose his HIV status. In May of that year, he began a sexual relationship with P.D. He never used a condom and said nothing about HIV.

***

The state's expert, Dr. Johnson *** thought that it was significant that defendant agreed to use, and in fact used, condoms when having intercourse with a woman for whom he expressed affection, but he did not use condoms with the other women with whom he had sex. Johnson also reported a conversation with another of defendant's former sexual partners, who said that, although defendant had denied that he was HIV-positive, he said that if he were positive, he would spread the virus to other people. In Johnson's opinion, such statements, coupled with defendant's behavior, showed intentional, deliberate conduct. Particularly in the light of the pattern of systematically recruiting and exploiting multiple partners over a long period of time, Johnson said, he found no evidence to suggest that defendant was acting impulsively or without the intent to harm.

***

from *State v. Haines*, 545 NE 2d 834 (Ind: Court of Appeals, 2nd Dist., 1989)

***

On August 6, 1987, Lafayette, Indiana, police officers John R. Dennis (Dennis) and Brad Hayworth drove to Haines' apartment in response to a radio call of a possible suicide. Haines was unconscious when they arrived and was lying face down in a pool of blood. Dennis attempted to revive Haines and noticed that Haines' wrists were slashed and bleeding. When Haines heard the paramedics arriving, he stood up, ran toward Dennis, and screamed that he should be left to die because he had AIDS. Dennis told Haines they were there to help him, but he continued yelling and stated he wanted to *** "give it to him." Haines told Dennis that he would "use his wounds" and began jerking his arms at Dennis, causing blood to spray into Dennis' mouth and eyes. Throughout the incident, as the officers attempted to subdue him, Haines repeatedly yelled that he had AIDS, that he could not deal with it and that he was going to make Dennis deal with it.

***

MORE PRACTICE WITH NEGLIGENCE

Flannery O'Connor's "A Good Man is Hard to Find"

Flannery O'Connor's famous short story, "A Good Man is Hard to Find" tells of the tragic deaths met by a grandmother and her four family members caused, in part, by the grandmother's apparently well-intentioned conduct. After locating and reading a copy of this story, assume that both the Grandmother and June Star survive the attack. Would June Star have a case against the Grandmother for the harm she experienced as a result of the Grandmother's negligent conduct?

Review the rules concerning negligence on page 137, and write an essay analyzing each of the Grandmother's possibly negligent actions in terms of the four elements of negligence. For example, assume that her first negligent action consisted of smuggling the cat into the car after being asked not to. Did her duty to behave reasonably in avoiding danger to others require her to leave the cat at home? If you think having a cat in the car is dangerous, you might say so. On the other hand, perhaps it was only an issue of the other family members not liking cats. All we are told on the subject is that Bailey didn't like to arrive at a motel with a cat. So maybe there is no safety issue here. Then again, you might argue that if the grandmother had not been secretive about the cat, it might have been better secured and not have been in a position to cause an accident. As you can see, there is room for argument on both sides.

PG#?

BIGAMY

The Case of the Accidental Bigamist

While most crimes involve an easily identified victim, a malicious state of mind, and an articulable harm, this is not the case with all crimes. Bigamy—the crime of having multiple spouses at the same time—may be said to have none of those three elements. Where all involved parties are freely consenting adults, it is hard not only to portray any of them as a victim, but also to conceive of how society as a whole is harmed by their private arrangement. Nevertheless, the harsh treatment of bigamy is striking. Despite involving no inherent violence or threat to life, it is typically classed as a felony. This ranks it among crimes such as kidnapping, torture, rape, and murder and means that those convicted of it face dire barriers to employment, citizenship, and integration into society. Further, defenses that are usually available to other crimes, such as having made an honest mistake or having the victim's consent, in many governments count for nothing. That is, a woman who marries under the belief that her disappeared husband is dead or who thinks that her divorce was valid may be convicted of bigamy even if she has utterly convincing reasons for holding her mistaken beliefs. Bigamy appears on many lists of the most serious crimes. For example, the Immigration and Nationality Act forbids known bigamists from entering the country.

Please research the laws of bigamy and its relation to immigration to provide recommendations for Diana, a 66-year-old woman from Mexico who wants to apply for Lawful Permanent Resident status in the United States as her U.S. citizen son is sponsoring her. Her story follows.

Diana's Case

Diana married her husband Paul in 1971. Both are Mexican citizens and had lived in Mexico their whole lives up until that time. In 1982, Paul moved out of their home and their marriage and communication effectively came to an end, although they never legally divorced. Paul actually moved to a house only a few blocks down the street, so the two could not help but pass each other from time to time and saw many of the same neighbors constantly over the next few decades.

In 1998, Diana saw a chance to emigrate to the United States when a friend of her family named Joel, who was a U.S. citizen, offered to marry her. Since she had not spoken to or lived with her husband in 27 years, Diana assumed that their marriage would be considered legally ended. Diana has a fourth-grade education and is almost totally illiterate, so she was not relying on research to make this conclusion. Joel and Diana married in California in 1998, but Diana never initiated the process of seeking U.S. residency or any other immigration benefit. She was too nervous that the government would think she had married only for immigration purposes, which constitutes fraud. Nine months later, she decided to return home to Mexico and lost touch completely with Joel who is now of unknown location. They also never divorced legally.

It is now 2011, and Diana has an opportunity to apply for U.S. residency through means that are completely legal. However, to all appearances, it seems she is a bigamist, and a bigamist is absolutely barred from entering the United States. As she thinks about how best to proceed, her questions multiply exponentially:

1. Does she really have two husbands? Or does California law dictate that she only has one? If so, which one? Would the answer change if she could prove that she thought her first husband was dead? Would she have a realistic chance of proving that?

2. If she has two husbands, should she divorce Joel? How can she divorce him if he is in the U.S. and she is in Mexico and cannot enter the U.S. until after the divorce? Will Mexico even recognize her marriage with Joel, and if not, will she be able to get a divorce in Mexico? If it turns out that California says she has two husbands and Mexico says she has one, what next?

3. Will revealing her situation either to the authorities in the U.S. or in Mexico result in her being charged with a felony? Going to prison? Does it matter that her second marriage was 13 years ago and/or that she has had no dealings with her first husband (or her second husband!) since then?

4. Will divorcing one of her husbands, assuming it's possible, solve the problem? Will the U.S. admit a past bigamist if she has only one husband now?

5. If a divorce is not possible in California or in Mexico, is annulment a possibility in either place?

6. Will immigration authorities even know about Joel's existence if she doesn't ever mention him?

7. Can she face legal trouble for having married Joel with the intent to get residency through him?

It is probably close to impossible to find clear answers to all these questions, but do your best to find as much relevant information as possible. Use official government sites as much as you can, but advice/informational sites might play a role in your research as well. Try to find the most reliable of such information, and use it as a guide to point you toward more reliable sources. Remember that the web is full of advisors that do not actually know what they are talking about.

One possible way to organize your essay is to come up with two or three alternative plans of action for Diana. Each major section of your essay can be devoted to one of those action plans, explaining what she should do, what the possible consequences are, and what research supports your recommendation. Do not give any advice or express any opinions that you cannot back up with researched authority of some kind.

IGNORANCE OF THE LAW

High on the list of phrases that most people have heard without ever setting foot into a courtroom must be the expression, "ignorance of the law is no excuse." The idea, of course, is that a criminal will not be excused simply by saying, "I didn't know that what I did was illegal" because that would be a rather obvious and easy way for anyone to escape the consequences of any crime. In reality, the matter is a bit more complicated. In some situations and under some circumstances, ignorance actually can be an excuse. After considering the following scenarios, write a compare/contrast essay in which you explain how a court should decide when ignorance of the law will be accepted as an excuse.

One way to do this is to come up with your own rules or criteria for allowing ignorance to excuse a crime. Then, select a few scenarios where you think the excuse should be accepted and a few scenarios where you do not, and compare the scenarios with each other to support your decision.

Alternatively, you may do research to discover what kinds of rules traditionally determine when the excuse will be accepted and then compare some scenarios that feature excusable defendants with others that do not. If you choose this option, be sure to seek reliable sources and document them thoroughly.

In no case do you need to write about all of the following scenarios.

Scenarios

1. Anna believes that she is lawfully married, honestly unaware that in her state a person cannot consent to marry until the age of 18. Her supposed husband was only 17 at the time of their supposed marriage. Thus, their marriage is void. When testifying in court concerning another matter, Anna declares under oath that she is married. Later, the truth is discovered, and the government wants to charge her under the following law: "Anyone found to have knowingly provided false information while under oath is guilty of the felony of perjury."

2. Barbara has been using her neighbor's wireless Internet signal for the past six months without the neighbor's knowledge. She is unaware that the law forbids doing so. The law states, "it is a misdemeanor to use the wireless computer network of another person without that person's permission."

3. Chris honestly but incorrectly believes that the foreclosure on his house is invalid because his official notice of the foreclosure was not sent by certified mail. Under this belief, he enters his foreclosed home because he thinks he has the legal right to do so. The law states, "Anyone who enters a dwelling without invitation by the lawful owner commits a misdemeanor."

4. Diana forcibly takes her daughter to a gym and locks her inside for 24 hours because she refuses to exercise. Diana incorrectly believes that a law gives her, as a mother, the right to confine her child for up to 24 hours. In fact, no such law exists. The law she is thinking of gives her the right to confine her child for "a reasonable time." However, the law does state that "anyone who denies someone their personal liberty without just cause or authority is guilty of the crime of wrongful imprisonment."

5. Edgar knows there is a law that prohibits drinking on Sundays for everyone except government employees. Edgar works for a state university and thinks that makes him a government employee. However, the creators of the law were only referring to people who work directly for the administration of the government. When he is found drinking on Sunday, he is convicted for it.

6. Fiona violates a law she has never heard of, a law that prohibits renting to more than three people in a single-family home. In fact, this law has never been published in any way that would make it available to the general public.

7. Gerald owns twelve dogs and is aware of the following rather badly written law: "It is a misdemeanor to own an excessive number of pets. Anything more than eight cats is definitely considered excessive." This law has always been applied to control only ownership of cats, and so naturally, he assumes such a law has no importance to him. Unknown to him, one day the highest court of his state decides that the law is meant to apply to dogs as well as cats, that the reference to eight cats was just an example, and that the legislature never meant that cats were the only animals controlled. The next day, Gerald is charged with violation of the law.

8. Helga is not sure if it is legal in her state to operate her own lottery. She hires a lawyer who turns out to be incompetent and who tells her incorrectly that it is legal as long as more than 50% of the proceeds go to charity. Relying on his legal advice, she begins to operate her lottery and is arrested a month later.

9. Israel runs a booth at the weekly fair where he smashes U.S. quarters and imprints people's names on them. He is unaware of a law that states, "It is a federal misdemeanor to knowingly use a piece of U.S. currency in a way that has not been officially approved by the U.S. Treasury Department." He knows what he is doing with the coins, obviously, but he does not know whether the U.S. Treasury has officially approved such use. In fact, they have not.

10. Jonas has never heard of the law that requires anyone with a felony on his criminal record to register with the police department in any city to which he moves within 24 hours of arrival. For this reason, he fails to do so.

11. Katheryn does not know that it is illegal to keep a goat on the same property in which children under 12 years of age reside. She has a 7-year-old child and a goat on the same property.

12. Lawrence reads an official bulletin from the United States Citizenship and Immigration Service (USCIS), the government agency officially responsible for the regulation of immigration matters. The bulletin states clearly that it is not a crime to provide medical care or give lodging to an undocumented alien. In reliance on this bulletin, he spends five days offering medical care to undocumented aliens. A month later, the Supreme Court of the United States decided that the USCIS had overstepped its bounds and that its bulletin was invalid, that it was never legal to perform the mentioned activities. On the following day, Lawrence is arrested for his actions earlier in the month.

Chapter

14 | Writing about a Novel

CHARLOTTE BRONTË'S *JANE EYRE*

Jane Eyre tells the story of a young woman in the nineteenth century who, after a childhood full of emotional abuse and neglect, finds herself working as a governess in the home of brooding, mysterious Edward Rochester. Mr. Rochester is drawn to Jane's innocence, integrity, and faithfulness. Jane is overwhelmed by his attentions. But when her Cinderella-style romance leads to his marriage proposal, the whole thing comes crashing down. Chapters 26 and 27 give the details of the crushing surprise that threatens to overwhelm Jane and places her in a moral dilemma. If your class is not reading the entire novel, read these excerpts before continuing.

---

from *Jane Eyre*

by Charlotte Brontë

***

Our place was taken at the communion rails. Hearing a cautious step behind me, I glanced over my shoulder: one of the strangers—a gentleman, evidently—was advancing up the chancel. The service began. The explanation of the intent of matrimony was gone through; and then the clergyman came a step further forward, and, bending slightly towards Mr. Rochester, went on.

"I require and charge you both (as ye will answer at the dreadful day of judgment, when the secrets of all hearts shall be disclosed), that if either of you know any impediment why ye may not lawfully be joined together in matrimony, ye do now confess it; for be ye well assured that so many as are coupled together otherwise than God's Word doth allow, are not joined together by God, neither is their matrimony lawful."

From *Jane Eyre* by Charlotte Bronte, 1847.

He paused, as the custom is. When is the pause after that sentence ever broken by reply? Not, perhaps, once in a hundred years. And the clergyman, who had not lifted his eyes from his book, and had held his breath but for a moment, was proceeding: his hand was already stretched towards Mr. Rochester, as his lips unclosed to ask, "Wilt thou have this woman for thy wedded wife?"—when a distinct and near voice said—

"The marriage cannot go on: I declare the existence of an impediment."

The clergyman looked up at the speaker and stood mute; the clerk did the same; Mr. Rochester moved slightly, as if an earthquake had rolled under his feet: taking a firmer footing, and not turning his head or eyes, he said, "Proceed."

Profound silence fell when he had uttered that word, with deep but low intonation. Presently Mr. Wood said—

"I cannot proceed without some investigation into what has been asserted, and evidence of its truth or falsehood."

"The ceremony is quite broken off," subjoined the voice behind us. "I am in a condition to prove my allegation: an insuperable impediment to this marriage exists."

Mr. Rochester heard, but heeded not: he stood stubborn and rigid, making no movement but to possess himself of my hand. What a hot and strong grasp he had! and how like quarried marble was his pale, firm, massive front at this moment! How his eye shone, still watchful, and yet wild beneath!

Mr. Wood seemed at a loss. "What is the nature of the impediment?" he asked. "Perhaps it may be got over—explained away?"

"Hardly," was the answer. "I have called it insuperable, and I speak advisedly."

The speaker came forward and leaned on the rails. He continued, uttering each word distinctly, calmly, steadily, but not loudly—

"It simply consists in the existence of a previous marriage. Mr. Rochester has a wife now living."

My nerves vibrated to those low-spoken words as they had never vibrated to thunder—my blood felt their subtle violence as it had never felt frost or fire; but I was collected, and in no danger of swooning. I looked at Mr. Rochester: I made him look at me. His whole face was colourless rock: his eye was both spark and flint. He disavowed nothing: he seemed as if he would defy all things. Without speaking, without smiling, without seeming to recognise in me a human being, he only twined my waist with his arm and riveted me to his side.

"Who are you?" he asked of the intruder.

"My name is Briggs, a solicitor of—Street, London."

"And you would thrust on me a wife?"

"I would remind you of your lady's existence, sir, which the law recognises, if you do not."

"Favour me with an account of her—with her name, her parentage, her place of abode."

"Certainly." Mr. Briggs calmly took a paper from his pocket, and read out in a sort of official, nasal voice:—

"'I affirm and can prove that on the 20th of October A.D.—(a date of fifteen years back), Edward Fairfax Rochester, of Thornfield Hall, in the county of—, and of Ferndean Manor, in —shire, England, was married to my sister, Bertha Antoinetta Mason, daughter of Jonas Mason, merchant, and of Antoinetta his wife, a Creole, at—church, Spanish Town, Jamaica. The record of the marriage will be found in the register of that church—a copy of it is now in my possession. Signed, Richard Mason.'"

"That—if a genuine document—may prove I have been married, but it does not prove that the woman mentioned therein as my wife is still living."

"She was living three months ago," returned the lawyer.

"How do you know?"

"I have a witness to the fact, whose testimony even you, sir, will scarcely controvert."

"Produce him—or go to hell."

"I will produce him first—he is on the spot. Mr. Mason, have the goodness to step forward."

Mr. Rochester, on hearing the name, set his teeth; he experienced, too, a sort of strong convulsive quiver; near to him as I was, I felt the spasmodic movement of fury or despair run through his frame. The second stranger, who had hitherto lingered in the background, now drew near; a pale face looked over the solicitor's shoulder—yes, it was Mason himself. Mr. Rochester turned and glared at him. His eye, as I have often said, was a black eye: it had now a tawny, nay, a bloody light in its gloom; and his face flushed—olive cheek and hueless forehead received a glow as from spreading, ascending heart-fire: and he stirred, lifted his strong arm—he could have struck Mason, dashed him on the church-floor, shocked by ruthless blow the breath from his body—but Mason shrank away, and cried faintly, "Good God!" Contempt fell cool on Mr. Rochester—his passion died as if a blight had shrivelled it up: he only asked—"What have YOU to say?"

An inaudible reply escaped Mason's white lips.

"The devil is in it if you cannot answer distinctly. I again demand, what have you to say?"

"Sir—sir," interrupted the clergyman, "do not forget you are in a sacred place." Then addressing Mason, he inquired gently, "Are you aware, sir, whether or not this gentleman's wife is still living?"

"Courage," urged the lawyer,—"speak out."

"She is now living at Thornfield Hall," said Mason, in more articulate tones: "I saw her there last April. I am her brother."

"At Thornfield Hall!" ejaculated the clergyman. "Impossible! I am an old resident in this neighbourhood, sir, and I never heard of a Mrs. Rochester at Thornfield Hall."

I saw a grim smile contort Mr. Rochester's lips, and he muttered—

"No, by God! I took care that none should hear of it—or of her under that name."
He mused—for ten minutes he held counsel with himself: he formed his resolve, and
announced it—

"Enough! all shall bolt out at once, like the bullet from the barrel. Wood, close your
book and take off your surplice; John Green (to the clerk), leave the church: there will be
no wedding to-day." The man obeyed.

Mr. Rochester continued, hardily and recklessly: "Bigamy is an ugly word!—I meant,
however, to be a bigamist; but fate has out- manoeuvred me, or Providence has checked
me,—perhaps the last. I am little better than a devil at this moment; and, as my pastor
there would tell me, deserve no doubt the sternest judgments of God, even to the quench-
less fire and deathless worm. Gentlemen, my plan is broken up:—what this lawyer and
his client say is true: I have been married, and the woman to whom I was married lives!
You say you never heard of a Mrs. Rochester at the house up yonder, Wood; but I dare-
say you have many a time inclined your ear to gossip about the mysterious lunatic kept
there under watch and ward. Some have whispered to you that she is my bastard half-
sister: some, my cast- off mistress. I now inform you that she is my wife, whom I married
fifteen years ago,—Bertha Mason by name; sister of this resolute personage, who is now,
with his quivering limbs and white cheeks, showing you what a stout heart men may
bear. Cheer up, Dick!—never fear me!—I'd almost as soon strike a woman as you. Bertha
Mason is mad; and she came of a mad family; idiots and maniacs through three generations? Her mother, the Creole, was both a madwoman and a drunkard!—as I found
out after I had wed the daughter: for they were silent on family secrets before. Bertha, like
a dutiful child, copied her parent in both points. I had a charming partner—pure, wise,
modest: you can fancy I was a happy man. I went through rich scenes! Oh! my experience has been heavenly, if you only knew it! But I owe you no further explanation. Briggs,
Wood, Mason, I invite you all to come up to the house and visit Mrs. Poole's patient,
and MY WIFE! You shall see what sort of a being I was cheated into espousing, and
judge whether or not I had a right to break the compact, and seek sympathy with something at least human. This girl," he continued, looking at me, "knew no more than you,
Wood, of the disgusting secret: she thought all was fair and legal and never dreamt she
was going to be entrapped into a feigned union with a defrauded wretch, already bound
to a bad, mad, and embruted partner! Come all of you—follow!"

Still holding me fast, he left the church: the three gentlemen came after. At the front
door of the hall we found the carriage.

"Take it back to the coach-house, John," said Mr. Rochester coolly; "it will not be
wanted to-day."

At our entrance, Mrs. Fairfax, Adele, Sophie, Leah, advanced to meet and greet us.

"To the right-about—every soul!" cried the master; "away with your congratula-
tions! Who wants them? Not I!—they are fifteen years too late!"

He passed on and ascended the stairs, still holding my hand, and still beckoning the gentlemen to follow him, which they did. We mounted the first staircase, passed up the gallery, proceeded to the third storey: the low, black door, opened by Mr. Rochester's master-key, admitted us to the tapestried room, with its great bed and its pictorial cabinet.

"You know this place, Mason," said our guide; "she bit and stabbed you here."

He lifted the hangings from the wall, uncovering the second door: this, too, he opened. In a room without a window, there burnt a fire guarded by a high and strong fender, and a lamp suspended from the ceiling by a chain. Grace Poole bent over the fire, apparently cooking something in a saucepan. In the deep shade, at the farther end of the room, a figure ran backwards and forwards. What it was, whether beast or human being, one could not, at first sight, tell: it grovelled, seemingly, on all fours; it snatched and growled like some strange wild animal: but it was covered with clothing, and a quantity of dark, grizzled hair, wild as a mane, hid its head and face.

"Good-morrow, Mrs. Poole!" said Mr. Rochester. "How are you? and how is your charge to-day?"

"We're tolerable, sir, I thank you," replied Grace, lifting the boiling mess carefully on to the hob: "rather snappish, but not 'rageous."

A fierce cry seemed to give the lie to her favourable report: the clothed hyena rose up, and stood tall on its hind-feet.

"Ah! sir, she sees you!" exclaimed Grace: "you'd better not stay."

"Only a few moments, Grace: you must allow me a few moments."

"Take care then, sir!—for God's sake, take care!"

The maniac bellowed: she parted her shaggy locks from her visage, and gazed wildly at her visitors. I recognised well that purple face,—those bloated features. Mrs. Poole advanced.

"Keep out of the way," said Mr. Rochester, thrusting her aside: "she has no knife now, I suppose, and I'm on my guard."

"One never knows what she has, sir: she is so cunning: it is not in mortal discretion to fathom her craft."

"We had better leave her," whispered Mason.

"Go to the devil!" was his brother-in-law's recommendation.

"'Ware!" cried Grace. The three gentlemen retreated simultaneously. Mr. Rochester flung me behind him: the lunatic sprang and grappled his throat viciously, and laid her teeth to his cheek: they struggled. She was a big woman, in stature almost equalling her husband, and corpulent besides: she showed virile force in the contest—more than once she almost throttled him, athletic as he was. He could have settled her with a well-planted blow; but he would not strike: he would only wrestle. At last he mastered her arms; Grace Poole gave him a cord, and he pinioned them behind her: with more rope, which was at hand, he bound her to a chair. The operation was performed amidst the fiercest yells and the most convulsive plunges. Mr. Rochester then turned to the spectators: he looked at them with a smile both acrid and desolate.

"That is MY WIFE," said he. "Such is the sole conjugal embrace I am ever to know— such are the endearments which are to solace my leisure hours! And THIS is what I wished to have" (laying his hand on my shoulder): "this young girl, who stands so grave and quiet at the mouth of hell, looking collectedly at the gambols of a demon, I wanted her just as a change after that fierce ragout. Wood and Briggs, look at the difference! Compare these clear eyes with the red balls yonder—this face with that mask—this form with that bulk; then judge me, priest of the gospel and man of the law, and remember with what judgment ye judge ye shall be judged! Off with you now. I must shut up my prize."

We all withdrew. Mr. Rochester stayed a moment behind us, to give some further order to Grace Poole. The solicitor addressed me as he descended the stair.

"You, madam," said he, "are cleared from all blame: your uncle will be glad to hear it—if, indeed, he should be still living—when Mr. Mason returns to Madeira."

* * *

Some time in the afternoon I raised my head, and looking round and seeing the western sun gilding the sign of its decline on the wall, I asked, "What am I to do?"

* * *

But the answer my mind gave—"Leave Thornfield at once"—was so prompt, so dread, that I stopped my ears. I said I could not bear such words now. "That I am not Edward Rochester's bride is the least part of my woe," I alleged: "that I have wakened out of most glorious dreams, and found them all void and vain, is a horror I could bear and master; but that I must leave him decidedly, instantly, entirely, is intolerable. I cannot do it."

But, then, a voice within me averred that I could do it and foretold that I should do it. I wrestled with my own resolution: I wanted to be weak that I might avoid the awful passage of further suffering I saw laid out for me; and Conscience, turned tyrant, held Passion by the throat, told her tauntingly, she had yet but dipped her dainty foot in the slough, and swore that with that arm of iron he would thrust her down to unsounded depths of agony.

"Let me be torn away," then I cried. "Let another help me!"

"No; you shall tear yourself away, none shall help you: you shall yourself pluck out your right eye; yourself cut off your right hand: your heart shall be the victim, and you the priest to transfix it."

I rose up suddenly, terror-struck at the solitude which so ruthless a judge haunted,— at the silence which so awful a voice filled. My head swam as I stood erect. I perceived that I was sickening from excitement and inanition; neither meat nor drink had passed my lips that day, for I had taken no breakfast. And, with a strange pang, I now reflected that, long as I had been shut up here, no message had been sent to ask how I was, or to invite me to come down: not even little Adele had tapped at the door; not even Mrs. Fairfax had sought me. "Friends always forget those whom fortune forsakes," I murmured, as I undrew the bolt and passed out. I stumbled over an obstacle: my head was still dizzy, my sight was dim, and my limbs were feeble. I could not soon recover myself. I fell, but not on to the ground: an outstretched arm caught me. I looked up—I was supported by Mr. Rochester, who sat in a chair across my chamber threshold.

"You come out at last," he said. "Well, I have been waiting for you long, and listening: yet not one movement have I heard, nor one sob: five minutes more of that death-like hush, and I should have forced the lock like a burglar. So you shun me?—you shut yourself up and grieve alone! I would rather you had come and upbraided me with vehemence. You are passionate. I expected a scene of some kind. I was prepared for the hot rain of tears; only I wanted them to be shed on my breast: now a senseless floor has received them, or your drenched handkerchief. But I err: you have not wept at all! I see a white cheek and a faded eye, but no trace of tears. I suppose, then, your heart has been weeping blood?"

"Well, Jane! not a word of reproach? Nothing bitter—nothing poignant? Nothing to cut a feeling or sting a passion? You sit quietly where I have placed you, and regard me with a weary, passive look."

"Jane, I never meant to wound you thus. If the man who had but one little ewe lamb that was dear to him as a daughter, that ate of his bread and drank of his cup, and lay in his bosom, had by some mistake slaughtered it at the shambles, he would not have rued his bloody blunder more than I now rue mine. Will you ever forgive me?"

Reader, I forgave him at the moment and on the spot. There was such deep remorse in his eye, such true pity in his tone, such manly energy in his manner; and besides, there was such unchanged love in his whole look and mien—I forgave him all: yet not in words, not outwardly; only at my heart's core.

* * *

"I must leave Adele and Thornfield. I must part with you for my whole life: I must begin a new existence among strange faces and strange scenes."

"Of course: I told you you should. I pass over the madness about parting from me. You mean you must become a part of me. As to the new existence, it is all right: you shall yet be my wife: I am not married. You shall be Mrs. Rochester—both virtually and nominally. I shall keep only to you so long as you and I live. You shall go to a place I have in the south of France: a whitewashed villa on the shores of the Mediterranean. There you shall live a happy, and guarded, and most innocent life. Never fear that I wish to lure you into error—to make you my mistress. Why did you shake your head? Jane, you must be reasonable, or in truth I shall again become frantic."

His voice and hand quivered: his large nostrils dilated; his eye blazed: still I dared to speak.

"Sir, your wife is living: that is a fact acknowledged this morning by yourself. If I lived with you as you desire, I should then be your mistress: to say otherwise is sophistical—is false."

"Jane, I am not a gentle-tempered man—you forget that: I am not long-enduring; I am not cool and dispassionate. Out of pity to me and yourself, put your finger on my pulse, feel how it throbs, and—beware!"

He bared his wrist, and offered it to me: the blood was forsaking his cheek and lips, they were growing livid; I was distressed on all hands. To agitate him thus deeply, by a resistance he so abhorred, was cruel: to yield was out of the question. I did what human beings do instinctively when they are driven to utter extremity—looked for aid to one higher than man: the words "God help me!" burst involuntarily from my lips.

"I am a fool!" cried Mr. Rochester suddenly. "I keep telling her I am not married, and do not explain to her why. I forget she knows nothing of the character of that woman, or of the circumstances attending my infernal union with her. Oh, I am certain Jane will agree with me in opinion, when she knows all that I know! Just put your hand in mine, Janet—that I may have the evidence of touch as well as sight, to prove you are near me—and I will in a few words show you the real state of the case. Can you listen to me?"

"Yes, sir; for hours if you will."

"I ask only minutes. Jane, did you ever hear or know that I was not the eldest son of my house: that I had once a brother older than I?"

"I remember Mrs. Fairfax told me so once."

"And did you ever hear that my father was an avaricious, grasping man?"

"I have understood something to that effect."

"Well, Jane, being so, it was his resolution to keep the property together; he could not bear the idea of dividing his estate and leaving me a fair portion: all, he resolved, should go to my brother, Rowland. Yet as little could he endure that a son of his should be a poor man. I must be provided for by a wealthy marriage. He sought me a partner betimes. Mr. Mason, a West India planter and merchant, was his old acquaintance. He was certain his possessions were real and vast: he made inquiries. Mr. Mason, he found, had a son and daughter; and he learned from him that he could and would give the latter a fortune of thirty thousand pounds: that sufficed. When I left college, I was sent out to Jamaica, to espouse a bride already courted for me. My father said nothing about her money; but he told me Miss Mason was the boast of Spanish Town for her beauty: and this was no lie. I found her a fine woman, in the style of Blanche Ingram: tall, dark, and majestic. Her family wished to secure me because I was of a good race; and so did she. They showed her to me in parties, splendidly dressed. I seldom saw her alone, and had very little private conversation with her. She flattered me, and lavishly displayed for my pleasure her charms and accomplishments. All the men in her circle seemed to admire her and envy me. I was dazzled, stimulated: my senses were excited; and being ignorant, raw, and inexperienced, I thought I loved her. There is no folly so besotted that the idiotic rivalries of society, the prurience, the rashness, the blindness of youth, will not hurry a man to its commission. Her relatives encouraged me; competitors piqued me; she allured me: a marriage was achieved almost before I knew where I was. Oh, I have no respect for myself when I think of that act!—an agony of inward contempt masters me. I never loved, I never esteemed, I did not even know her. I was not sure of the existence of one virtue in her nature: I had marked neither modesty, nor benevolence, nor candour, nor refinement in her mind or manners—and, I married her:- gross, grovelling, mole-eyed blockhead that I was! With less sin I might have—But let me remember to whom I am speaking."

"My bride's mother I had never seen: I understood she was dead. The honeymoon over, I learned my mistake; she was only mad, and shut up in a lunatic asylum. There was a younger brother, too—a complete dumb idiot. The elder one, whom you have seen (and whom I cannot hate, whilst I abhor all his kindred, because he has some grains of affection in his feeble mind, shown in the continued interest he takes in his wretched sister, and also in a dog-like attachment he once bore me), will probably be in the same state one day. My father and my brother Rowland knew all this; but they thought only of the thirty thousand pounds, and joined in the plot against me."

"These were vile discoveries; but except for the treachery of concealment, I should have made them no subject of reproach to my wife, even when I found her nature wholly alien to mine, her tastes obnoxious to me, her cast of mind common, low, narrow, and singularly incapable of being led to anything higher, expanded to anything larger—when I found that I could not pass a single evening, nor even a single hour of the day with her in comfort; that kindly conversation could not be sustained between us, because whatever topic I started, immediately received from her a turn at once coarse and trite, perverse and imbecile—when I perceived that I should never have a quiet or settled household, because no servant would bear the continued outbreaks of her violent and unreasonable temper, or the vexations of her absurd, contradictory, exacting orders—even then I restrained myself: I eschewed upbraiding, I curtailed remonstrance; I tried to devour my repentance and disgust in secret; I repressed the deep antipathy I felt.

"Jane, I will not trouble you with abominable details: some strong words shall express what I have to say. I lived with that woman upstairs four years, and before that time she had tried me indeed: her character ripened and developed with frightful rapidity; her vices sprang up fast and rank: they were so strong, only cruelty could check them, and I would not use cruelty. What a pigmy intellect she had, and what giant propensities! How fearful were the curses those propensities entailed on me! Bertha Mason, the true daughter of an infamous mother, dragged me through all the hideous and degrading agonies which must attend a man bound to a wife at once intemperate and unchaste.

"My brother in the interval was dead, and at the end of the four years my father died too. I was rich enough now—yet poor to hideous indigence: a nature the most gross, impure, depraved I ever saw, was associated with mine, and called by the law and by society a part of me. And I could not rid myself of it by any legal proceedings: for the doctors now discovered that MY WIFE was mad—her excesses had prematurely developed the germs of insanity. Jane, you don't like my narrative; you look almost sick—shall I defer the rest to another day?"

"No, sir, finish it now; I pity you—I do earnestly pity you."

* * *

"Jane, I approached the verge of despair; a remnant of self-respect was all that intervened between me and the gulf. In the eyes of the world, I was doubtless covered with grimy dishonour; but I resolved to be clean in my own sight—and to the last I repudiated the contamination of her crimes, and wrenched myself from connection with her mental defects. Still, society associated my name and person with hers; I yet saw her and heard her daily: something of her breath (faugh!) mixed with the air I breathed; and besides, I remembered I had once been her husband—that recollection was then, and is now, inexpressibly odious to me; moreover, I knew that while she lived I could never be the husband of another and better wife; and, though five years my senior (her family and her father had lied to me even in the particular of her age), she was likely to live as long as I, being as robust in frame as she was infirm in mind. Thus, at the age of twenty-six, I was hopeless.

* * *

"'This life,' said I at last, 'is hell: this is the air—those are the sounds of the bottomless pit! I have a right to deliver myself from it if I can. The sufferings of this mortal state will leave me with the heavy flesh that now cumbers my soul. Of the fanatic's burning eternity I have no fear: there is not a future state worse than this present one—let me break away, and go home to God!'

"I said this whilst I knelt down at, and unlocked a trunk which contained a brace of loaded pistols: I mean to shoot myself. I only entertained the intention for a moment; for, not being insane, the crisis of exquisite and unalloyed despair, which had originated the wish and design of self-destruction, was past in a second.

* * *

"'Go,' said Hope, 'and live again in Europe: there it is not known what a sullied name you bear, nor what a filthy burden is bound to you. You may take the maniac with you to England; confine her with due attendance and precautions at Thornfield: then travel yourself to what clime you will, and form what new tie you like. That woman, who has so abused your long-suffering, so sullied your name, so outraged your honour, so blighted your youth, is not your wife, nor are you her husband. See that she is cared for as her condition demands, and you have done all that God and humanity require of you. Let her identity, her connection with yourself, be buried in oblivion: you are bound to impart them to no living being. Place her in safety and comfort: shelter her degradation with secrecy, and leave her.'

"I acted precisely on this suggestion. My father and brother had not made my marriage known to their acquaintance; because, in the very first letter I wrote to apprise them of the union—having already begun to experience extreme disgust of its consequences, and, from the family character and constitution, seeing a hideous future opening to me—I added an urgent charge to keep it secret: and very soon the infamous conduct of the wife my father had selected for me was such as to make him blush to own her as his daughter-in-law. Far from desiring to publish the connection, he became as anxious to conceal it as myself.

"To England, then, I conveyed her; a fearful voyage I had with such a monster in the vessel. Glad was I when I at last got her to Thornfield, and saw her safely lodged in that third-storey room, of whose secret inner cabinet she has now for ten years made a wild beast's den—a goblin's cell. I had some trouble in finding an attendant for her, as it was necessary to select one on whose fidelity dependence could be placed; for her ravings would inevitably betray my secret: besides, she had lucid intervals of days—sometimes weeks—which she filled up with abuse of me. At last I hired Grace Poole from the Grimsby Retreat. She and the surgeon, Carter (who dressed Mason's wounds that night he was stabbed and worried), are the only two I have ever admitted to my confidence. Mrs. Fairfax may indeed have suspected something, but she could have gained no precise knowledge as to facts. Grace has, on the whole, proved a good keeper; though, owing partly to a fault of her own, of which it appears nothing can cure her, and which is incident to her harassing profession, her vigilance has been more than once lulled and baffled. The lunatic is both cunning and malignant; she has never failed to take advantage of her guardian's temporary lapses; once to secrete the knife with which she stabbed her brother, and twice to possess herself of the key of her cell, and issue therefrom in the night-time. On the first of these occasions, she perpetrated the attempt to burn me in my bed; on the second, she paid that ghastly visit to you. I thank Providence, who watched over you, that she then spent her fury on your wedding apparel, which perhaps brought back vague reminiscences of her own bridal days: but on what might have happened, I cannot endure to reflect. When I think of the thing which flew at my throat this morning, hanging its black and scarlet visage over the nest of my dove, my blood curdles.

"And what, sir," I asked, while he paused, "did you do when you had settled her here? Where did you go?"

"What did I do, Jane? I transformed myself into a will-o'-the-wisp. Where did I go? I pursued wanderings as wild as those of the March- spirit. I sought the Continent, and went devious through all its lands. My fixed desire was to seek and find a good and intelligent woman, whom I could love: a contrast to the fury I left at Thornfield—"

"But you could not marry, sir."

"I had determined and was convinced that I could and ought. It was not my original intention to deceive, as I have deceived you. I meant to tell my tale plainly, and make my proposals openly: and it appeared to me so absolutely rational that I should be considered free to love and be loved, I never doubted some woman might be found willing and able to understand my case and accept me, in spite of the curse with which I was burdened."

***

"You see now how the case stands—do you not?" he continued. "After a youth and manhood passed half in unutterable misery and half in dreary solitude, I have for the first time found what I can truly love—I have found you. You are my sympathy—my better self—my good angel. I am bound to you with a strong attachment. I think you good, gifted, lovely: a fervent, a solemn passion is conceived in my heart; it leans to you, draws you to my centre and spring of life, wraps my existence about you, and, kindling in pure, powerful flame, fuses you and me in one.

"It was because I felt and knew this, that I resolved to marry you. To tell me that I had already a wife is empty mockery: you know now that I had but a hideous demon. I was wrong to attempt to deceive you; but I feared a stubbornness that exists in your character. I feared early instilled prejudice: I wanted to have you safe before hazarding confidences. This was cowardly: I should have appealed to your nobleness and magnanimity at first, as I do now—opened to you plainly my life of agony—described to you my hunger and thirst after a higher and worthier existence—shown to you, not my RESOLUTION (that word is weak), but my resistless BENT to love faithfully and well, where I am faithfully and well loved in return. Then I should have asked you to accept my pledge of fidelity and to give me yours. Jane—give it me now."

A pause.

"Why are you silent, Jane?"

I was experiencing an ordeal: a hand of fiery iron grasped my vitals. Terrible moment: full of struggle, blackness, burning! Not a human being that ever lived could wish to be loved better than I was loved; and him who thus loved me I absolutely worshipped: and I must renounce love and idol. One drear word comprised my intolerable duty—"Depart!"

"Jane, you understand what I want of you? Just this promise—'I will be yours, Mr. Rochester.'"

"Mr. Rochester, I will NOT be yours."

Another long silence.

"Jane!" recommenced he, with a gentleness that broke me down with grief, and turned me stone-cold with ominous terror—for this still voice was the pant of a lion rising—"Jane, do you mean to go one way in the world, and to let me go another?"

"I do."

"Jane" (bending towards and embracing me), "do you mean it now?"

"I do."

"And now?" softly kissing my forehead and cheek.

"I do," extricating myself from restraint rapidly and completely.

"Oh, Jane, this is bitter! This—this is wicked. It would not be wicked to love me."

"It would to obey you."

A wild look raised his brows—crossed his features: he rose; but he forebore yet. I laid my hand on the back of a chair for support: I shook, I feared—but I resolved.

"One instant, Jane. Give one glance to my horrible life when you are gone. All happiness will be torn away with you. What then is left? For a wife I have but the maniac upstairs: as well might you refer me to some corpse in yonder churchyard. What shall I do, Jane? Where turn for a companion and for some hope?"

"Do as I do: trust in God and yourself. Believe in heaven. Hope to meet again there."

"Then you will not yield?"

"No."

"Then you condemn me to live wretched and to die accursed?" His voice rose.

"I advise you to live sinless, and I wish you to die tranquil."

"Then you snatch love and innocence from me? You fling me back on lust for a passion—vice for an occupation?"

"Mr. Rochester, I no more assign this fate to you than I grasp at it for myself. We were born to strive and endure—you as well as I: do so. You will forget me before I forget you."

"You make me a liar by such language: you sully my honour. I declared I could not change: you tell me to my face I shall change soon. And what a distortion in your judgment, what a perversity in your ideas, is proved by your conduct! Is it better to drive a fellow-creature to despair than to transgress a mere human law, no man being injured by the breach? for you have neither relatives nor acquaintances whom you need fear to offend by living with me?"

This was true: and while he spoke my very conscience and reason turned traitors against me, and charged me with crime in resisting him. They spoke almost as loud as Feeling: and that clamoured wildly. "Oh, comply!" it said. "Think of his misery; think of his danger—look at his state when left alone; remember his headlong nature; consider the recklessness following on despair—soothe him; save him; love him; tell him you love him and will be his. Who in the world cares for YOU? or who will be injured by what you do?"

Still indomitable was the reply—"I care for myself. The more solitary, the more friendless, the more unsustained I am, the more I will respect myself. I will keep the law given by God; sanctioned by man. I will hold to the principles received by me when I was sane, and not mad—as I am now. Laws and principles are not for the times when there is no temptation: they are for such moments as this, when body and soul rise in mutiny

> against their rigour; stringent are they; inviolate they shall be. If at my individual con-
> venience I might break them, what would be their worth? They have a worth—so I have
> always believed; and if I cannot believe it now, it is because I am insane—quite insane:
> with my veins running fire, and my heart beating faster than I can count its throbs. Pre-
> conceived opinions, foregone determinations, are all I have at this hour to stand by: there
> I plant my foot." ***

BIGAMY

Even though its heroine shrinks in horror from the idea of wedding
Mr. Rochester once his secret is revealed, it is possible to read *Jane Eyre* as
a powerful argument against the injustice of bigamy laws. Unlike many
other rules of law, the position on bigamy has undergone almost no
change since the publication of this novel in 1847. Are there logical reasons, compelling public policies, or humanistic considerations that support
their continuing existence? Or is it merely one of the most egregious
examples of the law's extreme resistance to change and modernization?

Write an essay presenting both sides of the argument: should bigamy
laws continue in their present form? When writing the "Keep anti-bigamy
laws" side, use your own ideas, logic, and research. But when writing the
"Abolish anti-bigamy laws" view, explain how *Jane Eyre* presents the case
rather than using your own arguments. That is, show how the story and
Mr. Rochester present compelling reasons to feel that anti-bigamy laws
are unjust, unuseful, and oppressive. Don't forget, when considering the
characters' options and decisions, that these events took place in the first
half of the nineteenth century. One thing, among others, that you might
consider: despite what she says, is even Jane sure that refusing the marriage is the morally right thing to do?

RELIABILITY OF TESTIMONY

Many readers of *Jane Eyre* have speculated that Bertha Mason was not
truly insane at the time of her marriage to Rochester, and that she was
driven insane by her husband's cruel treatment when he found himself
unable to accept and understand her culturally different behaviors. After
all, Bertha was from the West Indies and was marrying a member of a
highly repressive and xenophobic society. The novel suggests that
Rochester is extremely used to his authority and seems drawn to Jane's

demureness. Could it be that his wife's assertiveness, loudness, or strong will were what induced him to label her as insane? Reviewing his "testimony"—the account that he gives to Jane—look for evidence of suspicious vagueness. At times, his testimony seems deliberately to omit important details and gives ample room for the interpretation just described. Write an essay in which you argue that a reader of Rochester's testimony could fairly conclude that Rochester himself drove his wife insane when she failed to conform to his expectations.

INTENTIONAL INFLICTION OF EMOTIONAL DISTRESS

Courts historically resisted the idea of a lawsuit for the infliction of emotional distress, fearful of the potential for a flood of frivolous complaints. However, it is now possible to recover damages for such a claim when the following elements are present: 1) the defendant acts intentionally or recklessly; 2) the defendant's actions are extreme and outrageous; 3) those actions cause severe emotional distress in the plaintiff.

How successful would Jane be in suing Rochester for Intentional Infliction of Emotional Distress? He says repeatedly that he never intended to deceive her. Is this believable, and even if it is, could we not say that he acted recklessly, knowing that there was a real risk of harm to her but ignoring it? Do the reactions of others seem to show that Rochester's actions were considered outrageous in his community? Is there sufficient evidence in the text to show that Jane's distress was severe?

As an alternative writing assignment, consider the possible case of Mason v. Rochester. If our theories in the section titled "Reliability of Testimony" can be believed, Rochester effectively drove Ms. Mason insane. Could his actions here be seen as intentional or reckless? Extreme and outrageous? What would Rochester say in his defense, and how well would it be received?

Chapter

15 Writing about Film

TIPS FOR WRITING ABOUT FILM

When asked to write about a film, it is important to demonstrate an understanding of the complex and subtle ways that films manipulate their viewers to achieve a certain effect. Some of these methods are the same as those used by any form of communication, while others are unique to the medium of film. After reviewing a few suggestions on how to analyze films' meanings and effects, you will be presented with a series of writing challenges based on legal issues that arise in films.

Content

As with any written form of literature, your starting point will probably be a consideration of the events that transpire and the words that are said. When dealing with a film based on a true story, it is also important to ask what facts the writer has changed, what has been left out, and what has been given a different emphasis from what a non-entertainment-focused piece might have included. Even beyond these considerations, remember that a filmmaker has a vast array of other tools used to "steer" the viewer in an intended direction. A sophisticated response will take these into account.

Actors

Dialogue is dead on the page until the actor makes conscious decisions about how to express the lines and supplement them with nonverbal communication. Consider also the physical appearance of the actors, their clothes and makeup, as well as their basic physiological characteristics, which have been carefully selected by casting directors. Even a character's hairstyle (and changes that it undergoes) is often significant. One stereotypical example might be the repressed woman who signals her new-found liberation by letting her hair down.

Camera

A film is not like a play. The camera, not our eye, decides what we will see and how much emphasis we will give it. Consider what has been included within the visible frame and what has been excluded. Notice the angles from which we are shown the action, the movement of the camera, and the length of time between breaks in the filming (a continuous sequence of filming is known as a shot). Beyond merely noticing these things, however, be prepared to discuss what particular effect they might have. A high camera angle looking down might suggest a lurking predator, while a shaky camera could suggest chaos.

Editing

Even after story and dialogue have all been finalized, there still remain the decisions of what order to put everything in, how to connect the scenes, and how often to change scenes. Adjoining scenes often are positioned so that one or both makes some sort of comment on the other, suggesting parallels or contrasts. Our sense of how much time is passing can be determined by an editor's decision about how to pace the sequencing of scenes.

Effects

When it comes to effects, think not only of impressive special effects, but also of music, lighting techniques, and background sounds. A particular choice of music, for example, can drastically affect how the audience will respond to a certain scene. It is difficult to maintain a favorable attitude as ominous music plays, whereas lighthearted music encourages the audience to overlook any darker innuendos.

EMPLOYMENT LAW

The Devil Wears Prada

Many people are quick to sue their employers for what they term a "hostile work environment," but this concept is not very well understood. As with everything else, certain criteria have to be met to establish such a claim, the most problematic being that the hostility in question must take the form of discrimination toward a protected class of people. Traditionally, protected classes have been defined along lines such as gender, age, race, or disability. In other words, if an employer is not engaging an offensive or abusive behavior in the form of discrimination, then no matter how unpleasant the workplace, there is no hostile work environment. Of course, exceptions exist.

The Devil Wears Prada (2006) is a comedic film that tells of Andrea Sachs's ordeal in working for her despicable boss, Miranda Priestly. After viewing the film, do research to determine whether Andrea could prevail in a lawsuit against Miranda for creating a hostile work environment. It may appear from the preliminary definition we have seen that she could not, but don't give up so easily. For example, much of Miranda's abusiveness is either directly or could be seen as indirectly related to Andrea's supposed fatness. Can obesity qualify a person as a protected class? A little research will show that this has been open to debate. So perhaps Andrea can build a case that she has been the object of "weight discrimination."

Write an essay in which you research and present the required elements of a "hostile work environment suit," and use examples from the film to argue as to whether Andrea could prevail in such a suit. You may or may not want to research what has been said on weight discrimination and use that as part of your argument. As much as possible, try to focus on information that is valid in New York.

FAMILY LAW

Muriel's Wedding

When a divorce turns ugly, parents often try to vilify each other in an attempt to win custody of the children. Each parent may try to portray the other as unfit. However, this is usually very difficult to prove. Every state has its own criteria. In the film *Muriel's Wedding* both parents have fairly exceptional problems, and perhaps each of them could raise arguments as to why the other is unfit. Do some research to find out the laws regarding unfit parents in your state. Then use the criteria you find to analyze whether Betty, Bill, or both would be classified as unfit parents.

INSANITY

Should a killer be able to escape punishment by arguing that he was insane at the time of his acts? If part of punishment is based on the evil thoughts and intentions of a wrongdoer, then can we still fairly punish someone whose actions were not the products of his own free will? Different groups have come up with different answers, and even where it is agreed that an insanity defense is possible, standards of how to define insanity differ.

Heavenly Creatures

In the film *Heavenly Creatures* (1994), young Pauline and Juliet become desperate when their families attempt to separate them, and events culminate in their brutal, planned slaying of Pauline's mother. This gruesome story is based on real-life events, and in fact, both Pauline and Juliet attempted to enter insanity defenses which were rejected. Should they have been?

Please ***research*** the ***definitions*** of the insanity defense in our state and do some research to come up with ***examples*** of when it is accepted and when it is not accepted. Then, ***argue*** whether Juliet or Pauline (discuss them separately) would qualify by examining their actions and words. There are many ways to complete this assignment. You might focus on what the law itself says about the defense of insanity, or you might look for discussions of past criminals who successfully or unsuccessfully used an insanity defense.

Make sure that your sources are of high quality, that you attribute credit to them with parenthetical citations, and that you list them correctly in a Works Cited list.

Some possible questions you might want to focus on: Did the girls seem capable of distinguishing reality from fantasy? Did they seem to think and act in a manner that was at all logical? Did they seem to know that what they were doing was considered wrong by society's standards? By their own standards? What does the film do (in terms of acting, music, lighting, and editing) to reinforce your answers to any of the above?

Flannery O'Connor's "A Good Man is Hard to Find"

Flannery O'Connor's famous short story, "A Good Man is Hard to Find" introduces a dangerous criminal named The Misfit, who effects the killing of an entire family of five. If arrested, does he have any chance at escaping or reducing his sentence by reason of insanity? After locating and reading a copy of this story, please ***research*** the ***definitions*** of the insanity defense in our state and do some research to come up with ***examples*** of when it is accepted and when it is not accepted. Then ***argue*** whether the Misfit would qualify by examining both his actions and his words. There are many ways to complete this assignment. You might focus on what the law itself says about the defense of insanity, or you might look for discussions of past criminals who successfully or unsuccessfully used an insanity defense.

Make sure that your sources are of high quality, that you attribute credit to them with parenthetical citations, and that you list them correctly in a Works Cited list.

Some possible questions you might want to focus on: Does the Misfit seem to know what he's doing? Does he know what he's doing is wrong? Does he have a loose grasp of reality, and did that cause him to kill the family? How coherent and logical is he?

Make sure that your answer is based on legal definitions of insanity that you research and not just on your gut reaction as to whether he seems insane.

SEXUAL OFFENSES

Notes on a Scandal

Double standards have almost always worked to the disadvantage of women, but there has been at least one major exception. When it comes to crimes involving sexual misconduct with minors—at least where teenagers are concerned—male perpetrators have traditionally received by far the worse treatment. The male child molester is perceived as a monster, a dangerous predator who must be tagged and isolated from respectable society for the rest of his days. Many times, however, the same crime when committed by a woman is popularly regarded as a good joke. The perpetrator in these cases is seen as more ridiculous than monstrous, while the victim is typically portrayed as unscathed or even as deserving of admiration. Belief in equal treatment of the sexes would seem to demand the end of this double standard—that is, equal reaction and equal punishment regardless of the perpetrator's gender. But another philosophy might argue that gender does matter, and that it is not good sense to insist that sexual relations with a minor initiated by an adult male are of the same significance as those initiated by an adult female.

What position does the film *Notes on a Scandal* take on this issue? This film tells the story of 41-year-old Sheba, who finds herself embroiled in a sexual affair with one of her fifteen-year-old students. Does the film seem to paint her as a heroine, a victim, or a villain? Does the role of Barbara's character affect the way we perceive Sheba's problems? Do we ever get a convincing account of why Sheba does what she does? What does the film do to help us side with or against Sheba?

Another interesting writing assignment involves responding to the same questions in reference to the original novel of the same name. How does the film manipulate its audience toward different ends than does the novel?

MURDER

Scotland, PA

The film *Scotland, PA* (2001) tells the story of Joe (Mac) and Pat Mcbeth, a working class couple who become overwhelmed with greed and decide to murder their boss at the fast food restaurant where they both work. However, a rather bizarre chain of events leaves it doubtful exactly what crimes each could be charged with. Did Mac truly enter the restaurant with intentions of killing, or was Pat the only one with those ideas? In the end, was Duncan's death accidental? Can Pat really be said to have helped her husband in the killing of Banko?

Your purpose for this essay is to argue the innocence or guilt of the characters in *Scotland, PA*. You should emphasize innocence OR guilt for each issue you choose to discuss, but a good argument ALWAYS presents the arguments of the opposing side and then argues against them. Make sure you do so. It's your choice as to how many issues to write about, and you could well choose just one.

The legal rules that apply to murder can be found on page 169–171. You may do research to explore more about the law in this area, but be sure to document your sources if you do. Here are some of the possible issues your essay might take on:

- Did Mac kill Duncan with intent to kill?
- Did Mac kill Duncan with intent to cause serious bodily harm?
- Did Mac kill Duncan with reckless endangerment?
- Did Mac's killing of Duncan qualify as murder under the felony-murder rule?
- If Mac's killing of Duncan was murder, was it first or second degree?
- If Mac's killing of Banko was murder, was it first or second degree?
- Was Pat an accomplice in Duncan's murder?
- Was Pat an accomplice in Banko's murder as one of the consequences of Duncan's murder?
- Was Pat an accomplice in Banko's murder because she aided it?

INTENTIONAL TORTS

Definition of intentional torts

A tort is a civil wrong, which is to say it is a harmful action that does not rise to the level of a crime, one that can lead a court to compensate the victim by ordering the actor to pay monetary damages. There are a number of torts that can be actionable when they are committed intentionally. Some of the more common are battery, intentional infliction of emotional distress, trespass to chattel, and conversion.

Battery occurs when one person harmfully or offensively makes physical contact with another with the intent to make contact. It doesn't matter if the defendant wasn't trying to be harmful or offensive; a defendant who had the intent to make contact will be responsible for the results. Direct contact from one body to the other is not necessary either. Throwing an object at someone or grabbing something out of a person's hand could be a battery.

Trespass to Chattel occurs when one person interferes with another person's enjoyment or possession of a specific piece of personal property (known as chattel). The interference can consist of damage to the item, even if slight; taking possession of someone else's personal property for even just a few seconds qualifies as well.

Conversion is a more serious form of trespass to chattel and occurs when a person interferes with another person's enjoyment or possession of a specific piece of personal property to such a severe extent that paying for the item is the only acceptable remedy. This would be the case, for example, if the item were destroyed or never returned or even retained for an unacceptably long time. To decide whether there has been a trespass to chattel or a conversion, courts may look at factors such as: 1) the length of time the owner was deprived, 2) the amount of damage to the object, 3) the innocent or malicious intentions of the taker, 4) the amount of inconvenience caused, and 5) the possibility of undoing the damage to the object.

Intentional Inflection of Emotional Distress is another intentional tort, described in detail on page 197 of this book.

Defenses to intentional torts

A person who is sued for an intentional tort can begin their response by denying that the necessary elements are present. For example, she might deny that she had any intent to cause contact with the plaintiff or that events happened in the way that the plaintiff claims. Beyond simply trying to negate the plaintiff's side of the story, however, she can also raise what are called affirmative defenses. These may be thought of as excuses or justifications that, if believed, should remove responsibility from the defendant.

Self-defense can be claimed if the defendant was trying to prevent imminent bodily harm to herself. The requirement of "imminent" means that threats to cause harm in the future don't count. There has to be an immediate threat, a physical one. Furthermore, the defendant would have to prove that she was not the original aggressor. A person cannot start a fight and then claim self-defense when her opponent strikes back. An exception would be if the defendant had started a fight with non-deadly force, but her opponent responded with deadly force. In that case, the defendant could claim self-defense. One other requirement is that the defendant must only use the minimum force necessary. For example, if attacked with a rolled-up magazine, it is not acceptable for the defendant to respond with a gun. Doing so is said to exceed the scope of the self-defense claim and, therefore, render it void. This means that it is never permitted to respond with deadly force to any attack that was not itself using deadly force.

Defense of Others can be claimed if the defendant was trying to prevent imminent bodily harm to another person. As with self-defense, there must be an immediate threat, and the person being aided cannot have been the original aggressor unless she began the conflict with non-deadly force and met with deadly force in response. If the defendant thought that the person being aided had a legal right to assistance but turns out to be mistaken, she will still be able to claim this defense if she can convince the court that her mistake was reasonable.

Consent can be claimed it the defendant was acting with the plaintiff's permission. Disputes can arise as to whether a plaintiff really gave permission or merely appeared to do so. Consent is invalid if it is obtained by duress or certain kinds of fraud, and it is possible to exceed the scope of consent if the defendant goes beyond what the plaintiff has authorized.

The *Wizard of Oz*

This famous movie has occasioned an enormous number of interpretations, some serious, others silly. It has often been noted that, despite the innocence she exudes, Dorothy leaves a significant trail of destruction everywhere she goes. Is this a sign of repressed rage due to abandonment and a failed mother figure? Or perhaps it indicates a desire for more power from a girl who, in her own world, has none. For our purposes, we will concentrate on the legal aspects of what Dorothy does during the course of the movie. By the end, two witches are dead, the leader of Oz has been exposed and dethroned, and the entire power balance of the country has been altered because of Dorothy's adventures. If Oz were as litigious as our society, for what intentional torts could she be sued, and what might her offenses be? For example, did she commit a battery upon the Witch of the East or upon the Witch of the West? Was her possession of the ruby slippers a trespass to chattels, a conversion, or neither? You may consider other actions of hers as well, such as her taking of the witch's broomstick.

Write an essay in which you consider each of the suits that could be filed against Dorothy for intentional torts, explaining whether all the elements are in place and presenting Dorothy's defense against each. Be sure to present both sides of the argument before concluding which is the stronger side.

Index

S

T

U

W